SHAKING IT ROUGH

A Prison Memoir

SHAKING IT ROUGH

A Prison Memoir

Andreas Schroeder

Doubleday Canada Limited
Toronto, Ontario

Doubleday & Company, Inc.
Garden City, New York

1976

ISBN: 0-385-12310-8
Library of Congress Catalog Card Number: 76-17214

Parts of this book previously appeared in *Weekend* Magazine.

The excerpt from the Ronald McDonald Song
on pages 92-93 is reprinted with the permission of
McDonald's Restaurants of Canada Limited.

First Edition.

Designed by Robert Burgess Garbutt.
Printed and bound in Canada by
The Bryant Press Limited

*I wish to dedicate this book to Henry Beissel,
in whose Ayorama Cottage much of it was completed,*

*to Vern Dillabaugh, whose prompt and consistently
practical help proved invaluable time and time again,*

*and to all those friends who kept me afloat by
keeping in touch despite the censors.*

SHAKING IT ROUGH

A Prison Memoir

INTRODUCTION

When I confided in a fellow inmate that I was going to write a book about my prison experiences, he looked hopeful. "Fuckin' great," he encouraged, clapping me on the back. "That's the only way, man. If ya can't beat the buggers, at least ya can *understand* 'em to death." On another, later occasion he counseled me on what the book should contain. "Tell about the bitterness," he urged, almost as if he were arranging to smuggle a message to the Outside. "Make sure you tell about the bitterness. The fuckin' outrage, man."

At the time (just after I'd been incarcerated) the suggestion seemed to make sense; as far as I'd heard, that was exactly what prisons were all about—bitterness and outrage, a fundamental abuse of human rights and a malicious scrambling of the human psyche. Certainly the very architecture of the place heralded this; the great sullen towers, the puke-green concrete rabbit warrens, the steel bars and barriers endlessly crashing open and shut, the handcuffs, uniforms, strait jackets, cages and guns. There would be plenty of graphic examples to demonstrate the malevolence my cell mate was talking about—how could it be any other way? The sound effects alone were enough to convince me he was right.

Eight months later (after I'd been released on parole) I ran into the same terminology, the same point of view, on the *other* side of the fence. Following the publication of an article I'd written for *Weekend* Magazine on my prison experiences, I was overwhelmed with invitations to appear on talk shows, public affairs programs and the like, to "oh you know, describe some of the horrors of the place, the physical and psychic violence . . ." It was clear that what everybody was saying was "*Blame* somebody; make somebody *pay!*" I refused those invitations then, and now this book is in similar fashion a refusal to pound coffee tables with inverted oxfords or indulge in other such crowd-baiting tactics. Prison is simply *not* a face-off between long rows of malicious, sadistic uniformed guerrillas on the one side, and an equal length of deranged, slavering mother-raping murderers on the other. That may be how the two sides choose to see each other, but the true picture is much obscurer and sadder than that.

Prison is a huge lightless room filled with hundreds of blind, groping men, perplexed and apprehensive and certain that the world is full of nothing but their enemies, at whom they must flail and kick each time they brush against them in the dark. Prison is a bare and bewildering marketplace in which the sellers and buyers mill about in confusion, neither having the remotest idea of what to buy or what to sell. Prison is a composite of all those seats in the world which are obscured by pillars and beams, and from behind which you can see neither game nor scoreboard nor attract the attention of the ice-cream man.

All of which is not to say that there is no bitterness and outrage connected with prison; there is, and it is even on the increase. As more and more middle-class students and adults —who really *do* have something to lose—are being jailed for the sale or use of illegal drugs, the number of persons facing real tragedies in terms of their futures is growing at a frightening rate. In Canada's prisons, some 50 to 70 percent of all inmates are now doing time on drug or drug-related charges, and that percentage is going nowhere but up. In the '50s and '60s this was different; the average prisoner was relatively uneducated, even illiterate, and had never had any great career opportunities on his horizon in the first place. His incarceration wasn't really making any disastrously untoward dents in his future (as far as career is concerned) anyway. Nowadays, on the other hand, more and more corporate executive material (as Bay and Wall streets so kindly put it) is going to the dogs, and this "material" knows it well. What is worse, it knows it is paying the price for an overhasty, overheated and overblown reaction to an act (i.e., the ingestion of a drug) that will soon be taken off the lawbooks, and which is going to turn this incarceration into a complete waste, not to mention a penultimately tragic joke. It's hard to react with studied and unconcerned calm to such a fate.

However, this bitterness, while it exists *in* prison, is not directly concerned *with* it, but with the Law, and prison officials don't make the Law, they just carry it out. It happens, of course, that jailers sometimes carry out the laws a trifle too enthusiastically. But mostly the hostility we equate with prisons is in the final analysis an impersonal one, in which the jailer is simply the most handy representative of an intolerant society to which the inmate wishes to object (keeping in mind that we're only speaking about the perpetrators of victimless crimes: drugs, "immoral" acts such as prostitution, indecent exposure and so forth). Interestingly, those who have committed acts of violence or theft rarely complain about the Law at all. In most cases, they even *agree* with it, countering only with such knee-jerk excuses as "well, everybody does it; I was just the sad bugger that got caught." These inmates are generally not bitter as such, they simply see themselves as unlucky. At most, only about 10 percent of any prison population is what I would consider irredeemably and criminally short-circuited, people who have become so impassioned with the idea of causing destruction and mayhem that they are completely beyond practicable reach. And they're of course the people who always make the news.

Therefore it seems to me to be obscuring the issue to see "The Prison" as the essential Gordian knot in today's legal and moral perplex, although I don't deny that it's certainly the rather dramatic crossroads where all such difficulties happen to collide. What the *real* issue is, is the Law itself, and the fact that we don't even *understand* so-called deviant behavior to any extent, and that we have consequently not managed to come up with an effective way to deal with it. If I had intended to write a psychological or sociological treatise on this subject (assuming I were capable of it, which I'm not), those are the sorts of issues I would have busied myself with. As it is, however, this book has a more modest purpose, which is to describe a little of how it feels to be "treated" for such behavior by being imprisoned, and what such a life in prison is generally like. It is a personal account and makes no claim to being supremely objective, although it is also carefully and pointedly not a harangue; there has been too much of that already and it benefits no one. Needless to say, I have changed the names and some details pertaining to former cell mates in order to make them unrecognizable; but aside from such qualifications, all the incidents described in this book are true. There wouldn't be much point otherwise.

Andreas Schroeder
Mission City, B.C., 1976

The term *shaking it rough* is prison slang describing an inmate's inability to cope with life Inside, i.e., "doing hard time."

BACKGROUND

On May 5, 1973, as I was driving along a country side road toward Vancouver, B.C., a car ahead of me slowed and finally stopped directly in my path. The driver got out and came toward me; a quick glance into the rear-view mirror confirmed a second approaching vehicle blocking my retreat. By the time the first driver had reached my truck the second car was stopped behind and its driver out as well. I remember grinning a somewhat rueful grin, snapping off the radio and turning the engine off. "I guess that," I thought to myself as I pulled the ignition key, "is that." And so it was.

The count was possession of four pounds of cannabis resin (hashish) for the purpose of trafficking, and I received two years less a day for the offense.

FRAGMENT

1

Being arrested is a little bit like being told you have cancer. You know they wouldn't be saying it to you if it weren't true, and yet it doesn't seem to have an awful lot to do with you at the time. There is, of course, the matter of the slipped-on handcuffs and the police officer standing proprietorially close, but the import of all that doesn't really sink in until later, when it doesn't matter anymore anyway.

On that afternoon of May 5 there was no violence, no shouting, not even any show of unusual emotion; we might have been three drivers calmly discussing the insurance arrangements for a minor rear-end collision. The two presented their credentials politely and I heard myself answering almost amiably, accepting the documents as one gives a waiter the nod on a bottle of wine. My ears seemed slightly full of cotton and my mind a trifle loud but not noisy. I remember thinking, well there you are; the same damn thing every time you reach these places, these situations that are supposed to be the most dramatic you can find: finally making love to a woman you've wanted desperately for months or years; seeing someone killed before your eyes or seeing yourself about to be killed; finally achieving something that's been uppermost and urgent in your mind for too long—always, at the most climactic moment, it dwindles to the mundane, becomes simply normal and unsurprising. And you wonder what you really expected it to be: ecstatic? epiphanic?

One officer walked to the back of my truck and peered inside, the other spoke to me as if he were reciting memorized lines. I watched him very closely and wondered about his perfect-looking beard. He asked me to turn around and join my arms, then pulled my wrists together and snapped on the cuffs. The first officer had climbed into the truck and was digging around in the back. The other reached in through his car window and pulled out a black microphone into which he spoke a few commands, calling, as far as I could make out, for another squad car. Then he informed me he was taking my coat and wallet out of the truck, and was there anything else I might need in the Mission district lock-up? It all seemed very logical and sensible and a little unfortunate.

On the way to headquarters we passed a trio of youths trying to tow-start an old Chevrolet on a busy residential street. The officer driving stopped and called them over for a stern lecture on traffic laws and juvenile delinquency or something along that line; I only heard the first several words. The three stared into the car and I looked back, and for a few moments we were part of an automatic, almost conspiratorial unity, free and uncomplicated by the fact that we didn't even know each other and probably wouldn't have been particularly interested if we'd had the chance—content for that moment to assume the world divided into police and their actual or potential victims, and in some obscure way pleased to be part of the same assumption. There are police and there are the rest of us, the looks seemed to say; and if they'd just relax and forget about their phobia of wanting constantly to save the world from itself, why, they could be part of the rest

4

of the world too, and know everyone's secrets and passwords without having to use all these undercover power tactics to ferret them out. Then the lecture was over and the youths turned away, and suddenly I felt depressed for the first time that day. The unity was all very well, but now their difficulties were over and they were free to leave, while I felt the handcuffs tight across my wrist bones and realized that I had only just begun to confront mine. The squad car spun away, sliding me into the shoulder of the officer sitting on my right.

At headquarters I was taken into a small office and questioned for about half an hour, uneventfully. The young recruit assigned to take my fingerprints and mug shot couldn't unpuzzle the intricacies of the beautiful old Graflex camera set up in the Identification Room, so I took my own picture using the ten-second delay setting, giving him a quick lesson in photography as I set the mechanism up. Then the duty officer informed me I would be held incommunicado for forty-eight hours while my friends were investigated, after which a bail hearing would be arranged in due course. I was led to a gloomy little room that contained two empty cells and a very scarred-up toilet, and was locked into the cage nearest the door. Somebody stuffed an old blanket at me through the bars and the door slammed shut. I was, for the first time in my life, in jail.

FRAGMENT

Notes from the Mission jail cell: Recollected Thoughts

Of course there's the graffiti. They search you thoroughly, take absolutely everything from you except your pants and shirt and socks, and yet at least eighteen different people have managed to smuggle through some hard pointed object with which to scratch their names and comments into the painted steel plate of this cell's ceiling and walls.
ALAN MCCORMACK, FT. ST. JOHN. 3 YRS, ROBBERY; CORSONE, 5 MO. VIOLENCE WITH. FUCK EVERYBODY; JACK SCOLLER. KEEPS ON KEEPING ON. ESCAPE JAN. 7,73; ART G. 3 DYS. HAW HAW; PERCY MONTE, INUVIK. A ONE-PERCENTER.
Pictures of encircled crosses with three light rays where Christ's head would normally be—later I found out they're the symbol for incarceration; many inmates have them tattooed on their shoulders and arms. Surprisingly little sexual scrawling. The steel bunk is cold and there's only one blanket. I've asked them for another and they said they'd see.

*   *   *

I'm starting to lose my sense of time completely. There's virtually no outside light in here; the only window is a panel of thick glass brick which barely registers any light at all. What little light filters through seems entirely ambiguous; I can't tell whether it's morning or evening or lamplight. The disorientation is made complete by a small light bulb here inside that burns constantly. Strange, how damned annoying it is not to know the time of day.

*   *   *

In the door to this room there's a tiny inspection window, which somebody clicks open and shut every hour or so. I assume that's to make sure I don't hang myself. A few clicks ago I shouted toward the window that I'd like a few books to read, but there was no response. Last time the window opened I repeated my request and about ten minutes later the door thudded and rattled and opened to admit the young recruit who brought me three battered pocket books and lunch. The lunch wasn't so good but the book titles were marvelous considering the place I'm in: *Gang-Bang!* "the true story of a motorcycle gang's revenge on a woman who couldn't keep a secret!"; *She Stoops to Murder*: by Clinton Bolt ("she was a devil in disguise!") and *Attack*: Rommel's army smashes through the Sahara Desert. I've read them all and I must say I liked *She Stoops to Murder* best.

*   *   *

It's hard not to think about what's going on outside. I find I can't really stop myself from imagining the possible scenes, discussions, incidents (the papers must have reported the arrest by now); I imagine they'll have searched the house by this time too. Hope they haven't ripped everything to shreds. The worst feeling is having to lie here unable to *do* anything

7

about anything; and of course the mind persists in imagining the worst possible disasters out there. Must stop this line of thought entirely; it's pointless and corrosive. Unfortunately, there isn't much else to do in here but think. I've tried to play all those mind games I've heard about—prisoners playing solitaire from memory and such—but it doesn't seem to work. I suspect I haven't been here long enough to develop that kind of concentration; it's all still too new and there's simply too much that keeps interfering. I'm starting to realize just how much self-discipline it takes in order not to go uncomfortably frantic in a place like this. The only easily available antidote seems to be sleep.

*　　*　　*

The screen door is driving me strange. There's a corridor just outside the wall of this room which connects the parking lot with the front offices. At any time of day or night there's a steady stream of policemen tramping in or out through the screen door at the parking lot entrance. That door, which seems equipped with a retracting pump of some sort, shrieks slowly closed over a five-second interval every time it's opened. The policemen probably don't even notice it because they're always moving past it and don't have to listen to the whole routine, but I've been through it over a hundred times by now and I'm going nuts. The minute somebody begins to thump down the corridor I grab for my ears and press hard; that worked for a while, but now I find I'm beginning to *imagine* the sound despite my closed ears. According to what I suspect is a very rough estimate, I've been in here about forty hours. Another eight hours of shrieking door?

*　　*　　*

Now that was curious. The two narcotics agents who arrested me came "to visit" about an hour ago, and we had

8

ourselves a "nice chat." The two made themselves comfortable on the lower bunk and against the cell wall and asked if I was inclined to talk to them. I said sure, as long as they didn't expect me to answer any questions about the dope. They said that was fine and so we settled to the issue at hand as if we were sitting down to a game of chess, all three knowing exactly what was going on but everyone pretending otherwise. Each time the questions became anything but irrelevant I grinned and refused to answer, and they grinned and backed off for another try; it became a very absorbing game to determine the real intention of each question as it came. But what was even more intriguing was that I seemed to bear them no ill will at all. In fact, they appeared to me to be in some almost perverse way comrades in this strange adventure, and I even noticed in me the occasional urge to simply tell them everything they wanted to know as some sort of contribution to the cause, although what the cause might have been was entirely obscure to me. Of course I did nothing of the sort, but it did strike me as most peculiar and I thought about it for a long time afterward. I remembered then, dimly, that I'd heard about something like this before, about this odd complicity, this strange partnership between captor and captive, but I'd dismissed it at the time as one of those standard inversions of logic that are simultaneously enticing and improbable. Looking back on it now, I realize that the two agents were in all likelihood well aware that the phenomenon is often true, and were no doubt counting on that fact to make the interview worthwhile.

*　　*　　*

After forty-eight hours, my bail hearing. Shoeless and disheveled, I stand before the magistrate, hoping with more urgency than I care to admit that he's had a pleasant morning and an even better preceding night. He doesn't seem to notice

9

me at all, is more interested in my friend who has arrived to post the bail and the police officer who purportedly represents the Queen. The three dicker and deal and finally come to an agreement; then we all stand up and go through the same motions formally, as if the first negotiations have only been a dress rehearsal. My friend signs many forms and I sign many forms, and then the magistrate and the police officer sign the same, and finally it appears that one form is missing and the Mission RCMP office "has none in stock." I'm obliged to spend an extra day and night in my cell until the missing form is "found."

FRAGMENT

3

I was out on bail for nine months before my case actually came to court, but the interim fairly crackled with action. There were countless hearings, court appearances for pre-trial investigatory sessions, pre-sentence report interview, meetings with lawyers, prosecutors, police, witnesses; letters poured back and forth across the country accompanying applications, negotiations, agreements, repudiations, complaints, clarifications, documentary proofs, assessments, affidavits, petitions, court orders and the like. I saw my lawyer so often his offices began to seem like home and the secretaries soon all knew me by both name and sight. Anticipating a prison sentence (I was pleading guilty to the charge), I cast about for any information I could find on the subject; the results weren't exactly reassuring. "You only come out of those places in one of two ways," one person assured me; "either buggered in the ass or in a pine box." "They'll break your spirit like a dry twig," I was told. "You'll be marked for life in there; your responses will never be quite natural again." And, "They'll reprogram you like a tin computer." (One thing that has since become clear to me is that the majority of people, including the press, actually *want* these descriptions to be true; they *want* to hear that prisoners are having a bad time, that they are being punished or "paid back" for the crimes they've committed.)

When court day finally came I was apprehensive, to say the least, and soon had reason to be even more so: the prosecution had switched prosecutors at the last minute and all "understandings" reached through many pre-trial negotiations were suddenly in doubt. We had no idea as to what the new prosecutor had in mind.

Luckily he had very little, but what transpired during the proceedings disillusioned me in a way that only a trip to B.C.'s Parliament at the age of fifteen had heretofore managed to do, when I saw all the "honorable members" of our province's government behaving like spoiled children and couldn't believe my senses. At that time I returned home an abruptly evolved cynic, and after this court case my impulses were much the same. It was my first exposure to a peculiar brand of hypocrisy which I later encountered again and again in the prison system, and which to my mind is a major contributor to much of the failure of the Corrections Department throughout the country.

I'm speaking of this odd insistence on penitence, on remorse and contrition, which seems to be the stock-in-trade of parole boards, courts, religious Corrections groups and prison administrations everywhere; this odd insistence that an inmate must at all costs pretend not to be who he really is. The inmate, in effect, must plead remorse or be seen as unrehabilitated; if he makes this plea, his parole (or his pass or his reduced sentence or his application for transfer, etc.) is virtually assured. If he doesn't, there are very few boards that are not so rigidly committed to this mother/father-and-child routine ("Come on now; say you're sorry!") that they will not automatically defer his application.

The insincerity and (self) deception this engenders, even encourages, is both mathematically predictable and enormously far-reaching in its effect, and here lies the disaster of the prison system in a nutshell: our prisons are not "schools of crime" in the sense that mixing with "hardened criminals" teaches a new inmate new ways to blow a safe or forge a check (you don't have to go to prison to learn about that; there are books on the subject); they are schools of crime because they teach, they even force, an inmate to become a professional hypocrite in order to survive the place and get out. Because I hadn't then and I haven't since ever met an inmate who was sorry about anything except the fact that he got caught. But the constant fawning and lying required to negotiate the administrative, bureaucratic and psychiatric hurdles Inside are far more ruinous to his psyche than two years of beatings and hard labor might have been. Such hypocrisy is like the worst kind of disease; it spills over and infects an inmate's entire life, and when he finally gets out and tries to maneuver himself back onto the rails in Outside society, the automatic distorting and posturing has become a conditioned response which he finds virtually impossible to overcome, assuming he still wants to. Mostly, the attendant troubles of such situations aren't overly long in putting in their appearances, and in due course the vicious circle closes with a loud click.

In my court case, then, I was astonished to find this point belabored to an almost preposterous degree. I was presented as a contrite petitioner, a sadder but wiser young man, full of self-reproach and eager to make "amends" wherever possible. Since my attorney was an extremely able and intelligent/ articulate man, and since the judge seemed similarly bright, I had to assume that I was watching an old ritual which had become so well entrenched that even intelligent men could not do without it.

I might add that the prison term of two years less a day

13

which I was given was probably a reasonable sentence under the circumstances, given that we were still locked into the peculiar notion that smoking pot is a criminal offense.

After the trial, I was taken under guard to the Chilliwack municipal jail, where I stayed only long enough to be fed a lunch before being transferred to Oakalla Prison, Maximum Security.

FRAGMENT

I arrived at Oakalla Prison as part of a truckload of twelve, all of us handcuffed in pairs, nobody saying much as the truck jostled along (driver at the gate: "Got a dozen stiffs inna back, Gerry; I'll give ya an invoice for 'em soon's I get back."). The handcuffs were taken off at the Main Door, we were crammed into a tiny holding cell inside the Records Office and signed in one by one.

"All right! Name?"

"Truman. George Truman."

"Well, Truman, and what have we this time? Stealing pop bottles from infants is it? Ripping popsicle coupons off juveniles?"

"Naw, nuthin like that. Breakin an enterin, and theft. That's what they say, anyways, but I never done it, the bastards."

"Yeah, I know just what you mean, Truman; you and me both. Virgins like us have to stick together; they'll wipe us out otherwise. Want your old cell back, Four-Right-Eighteen?"

"Sure, I don't care."

15

"All right, you got it. Next!"

When I stepped up to the desk a guard frisked me from head to toe. Everything removable was removed; all rings, watch, belt, coins, shoelaces, wallet, lighter. The guard at the desk called them out one by one as he dropped them into a paper sack. I signed for the sack; he checked me out once more just to be sure. Then I was directed down a hallway to Identification, where I was fingerprinted, photographed and vitally statisticized.

Then it was mandatory showers and an issue of prison clothes; we stripped naked and handed our clothes to a flunky behind a counter who watched us without expression and signed for the clothes in return for a towel. We washed in an open shower room, then queued up farther along for the khaki-colored prison strip. The shirts and pants were heaped in huge hampers into which one simply grabbed at random and in a hurry; whatever you got was what you wore. My luck seemed on par with everyone else's; my shirt could have contained two of me and had only one button (on the sleeve); my pants were at least a foot too long and torn up both legs (although I later found out that was intentional). As I reached into the underwear bin an inmate on the other side of the counter hissed to attract my attention.

"Don't risk 'em, man," he whispered, imitating an itching crotch meaningfully. "Crabs, man, crabs."

I let the shorts fall back into the box and gave him the "compris" sign, although I was never sure afterward whether I had been had or not. All the shower stalls throughout the prison were loaded with bottles of a very potent evil-green looking disinfectant; it was virtually impossible to avoid the stuff. If there were any cases of crabs along our tier, I never heard of them.

My issue of prison boots was a similar disaster; we were trotted past a bank of old and banged-up working boots and told to call out our sizes, which we got if they were on hand,

16

or the closest size available if they weren't. The inside of mine had sharp nails sticking through in all sorts of places, a problem I eventually solved by twisting pieces of match-folder cover onto them.

Then it was off to the cells. The rooms and corridors echoed like swimming pools and the clash of steel rang in my ears like struck tuning forks. At Control, a guard handed me a slip of paper. "West Wing," he said and leaned over a control panel, pushing a button to open a grille covering the entrance to a connecting tunnel between the East and West cellblock wings. "And don't bend over without first lookin to see who's behind ya."

I walked slowly along the empty tunnel, a squared tube of thick, low-ceilinged, puke-green concrete, chamber after chamber interrupted by gate after gate, bars crashing as I presented my paper and passed on through. I could feel the knot in my gut now; I hadn't realized how tight my stomach had been feeling. Experimentally I let go a little and it started to flood in: numbness, nervousness, elation, fear, fascination. By god, I had to admit it was quite a place. This was vintage guerrilla theater; this looked like it was meant to grab you everywhere you lived; it didn't look like the sort of place in which you'd want to fall asleep. I started to whistle softly to myself, wondering just how and where I was going to fit into this scene.

"Hey you! Where the hell you goin?"

"Ah, West Wing, far as I know."

"Let's see that paper. Yeah, West Wing. Get your ass up those stairs to your left there."

I began to climb the stairs in question.

"And shut your goddamn yap before somebody shuts it for you. Nobody tell you you don't whistle in jail?"

As a matter of fact nobody had, though I suppose I might have known.

FRAGMENT

5

I was consigned to Four-Right-Sixteen: fourth floor, right tier (corridor), cell number sixteen. There was somebody in the top bunk already; I threw my blanket on the lower mattress and sat down.

"Who're you?" The face dropped upside down over the edge of the bunk.

"Name's Schroeder."

"Whaddya in for?"

"Dope."

"Far out."

"You?"

"Assault."

"Crazy."

"Name's Roster." A hand descended over the edge past the face.

"Pleased to meet ya, Roster."

FRAGMENT

There were forty-seven of us on that tier, two to a cell and you couldn't trade, but I was amazed how quickly we all banded together. We were an improbable bunch, everything from failure to pay alimony to attempted murder, we were Indians, Chinese, Hungarians, East Indians, Italians, you name it. We would probably never have given each other the time of day if we'd met on the Outside.

In here, it was a different story. It was us against them, not active warfare but a cold war, each side keeping as much to itself as it could. If communication was necessary you kept it short and loud; loud because secrets were dangerous commodities to have in prison. To be labeled a rat was the kiss of death; rats were stoolpigeons and they had something to hide. So the apparent antagonism between inmates and guards was rarely anything but impersonal, each person simply maintaining the party line for his own safety and comradeship. And if comradeship was essentially a pact between strangers to agree extravagantly on one or two items and forget the rest, we certainly had it made; a simple settling back on one's haunches and baying at the institutional moon, at the injustice, the oppression, the outrage, etc., invoked an instant clamor of agreement all around; one sat marvelously bathed in the wash of so much concord.

Even our speech reflected this will to solidarity. Cursing and general foul language was no accidental characteristic of prison jargon. When an inmate kicked irritably at an uncooperative piece of machinery and announced succinctly that "the fuckin fucker's fucked, fer fuck sakes!" he had neatly sandwiched two separate statements into one outburst; one direct (the machine malfunctions), one implied (jail is hell). He could always count on unanimous agreement because at least one of those statements was always correct, automatically ensuring safe passage for the other.

The guards, for their part, tacitly respected this solidarity in a very practical way; they never entered our rabbit warren in groups of less than three, and if an inmate was wanted by Administration for any reason, one of them simply cupped his hands and hollered through the entrance bars down the tier: "Sinclair! Four-Right-Nine!" I was quite startled the first time I heard that call, because after a brief silence a voice far down the tier distinctly hollered back: "You'll never take me alive, copper!" I quickly slid off my bunk to watch the ensuing hassle, but nothing happened and after a while Sinclair was summoned again: "Sinclair! Four-Right-Nine!" Later I found out that this was actually an old ritual, the inmate being summoned automatically hollering his defiance (which varied from the above to responses like "C'mon try and get me, asshole!" and "Try an' make somethin of it, bullmoose!") and settling back for the obligatory second call. That call having been made, and after a decent delay to indicate the appropriate lack of cooperation, the inmate would shuffle down the tier to be administrated unto.

So we spent our days not unpleasantly. Since none of us

had as yet been classified,* we could not be given regular jobs and so had a lot of time on our hands. While the cells were open (from 9:00 A.M. to 12:00 noon; from 2:00 P.M. to 4:30 P.M.; from 6:30 P.M. to 10:30 P.M.) we played chess or cards or read books; people drifted in and out spreading the daily rumors or joining the bull sessions that were always under way in one cell or another. At noon we queued up at the "kitchen hole" with our plastic cups and our spoons (no forks or knives permitted), picking up our trays from an unseen hand, which pushed them at us through a slot in the wall. The food generally consisted of potatoes (mashed) and starchy fodder, canned vegetables, salad (sometimes), some form of cheap meat (meat loaf, wieners, hamburger) plus canned or bakery dessert and coffee or tea or powdered milk. As a rule the food was overcooked to the point of falling apart but otherwise it seemed life-supporting enough. As soon as we had returned to our tiers the cells were locked, and we had to slip the emptied trays out under the cell doors for a flunky to pick up.

Two hours later they opened the drums again, and also a heavily fenced-in yard where we shot some of the best basketball games I've ever played. After yard came supper, then movies or gym or simply free time to write letters, read or sleep. Aside from the odd counseling or classification interview, or visits, there was no special claim on our time during those first few weeks.

Something that impressed me particularly at that time was the rapidity with which inmates seemed to unpack their psychic baggage before each other. With a casualness and

---

*When a man is first sentenced by the courts, he is automatically sent to the highest-security prison in the Corrections system. Once there, he is watched and interviewed, his record is analyzed, and if he is in consequence deemed sufficiently harmless and stable he is transferred (classified) to a lower security jail, sometimes right down to a minimum-security prison camp, which has no surrounding fence or cells. Unacceptable behavior in any minimum- or medium-security prison generally results in a reclassification back to maximum.

frankness that struck me as nothing if not quite dangerous, they exchanged confidences and intimacies within minutes of meeting each other, often before it even occurred to them to ask each other's names. It was a catching habit and somehow exciting; there seemed in all of us a willingness, almost an urge to throw away the old rules, a need in some strange way to celebrate our descent into this underworld with a reckless psychical potlatch. Instant friendships sprang up everywhere, alliances were forged and tested; it was all a little like having newly arrived in a foreign country, with new papers and a new name. There were many of us on that tier who had never been in jail before.

And yet, as I grew more accustomed to being Inside, I began to discern an underlying pattern that eventually alerted me to the survival techniques at play in this phenomenon. The older or more experienced inmates offered only "stock" or "standard" confidences, things (when you really looked at them) not particularly compromising at all, while the newcomers babbled away facts about former criminal acts, other contacts or friends, home addresses and information about their families—all of which the more experienced inmates quietly noted and "filed"; you never knew when you might need the edge over a man who at the moment was not being dangerous, but who could turn into an opponent as quickly as he'd become a friend. Many months later I watched one of these newcomers pay for such indiscretion when he was blackmailed by two lifers into using his visits to bring heroin Inside. As for myself, I learned very quickly to falsify enough details about my Outside life to make it improbable that I should meet any unwelcome ghosts from the past at my door. But if I didn't end up playing directly into someone's hands it was due to sheer luck rather than brains; of the standard list of newcomers' mistakes in prison (whistling in jail, talking to guards, obeying staff commands too promptly, admitting to all your job skills indiscriminately, answering all psychiatrists' questions truthfully, believing more than 10 percent of what you're told and putting non-coded information about your emotional state into letters to the Outside, etc.), I'm sure I committed most of them at one time or another.

And there was another phenomenon, which, concurrent with all our abandon, I could already see becoming increasingly defined: a hierarchy, a rigid pecking order was already relentlessly sorting itself out, eventually floating an elite to the surface which few challenged and even fewer successfully defied. By the time I had been Inside for a week, I had already developed an uncannily sure sense of where a newcomer would eventually come to rest on the social scale; in fact, most of us had done so. There was no distinct pattern to the selection, but one characteristic was unquestionably a major asset: if you clearly didn't *care*, if you could convince inmates and guards that you had absolutely nothing to lose and that your countermeasures to even the most trivial provocation would be totally unrestrained and pursued to the utmost of your abilities—then you were given respect and a wide berth, and people looked to you for leadership and advice. "He's crazy," they'd say admiringly, even longingly, when the name came up. "He's just totally, completely insane."

FRAGMENT

7

They call the man in Drum Number Eleven Coyote; my cell mate tells me he's an habitch.* He's alone in there and has nothing; he hasn't made the slightest attempt to get an extra blanket, untorn pillow or cardboard box for a table as most of us have done. He coughs a fair amount and sleeps as much, and every time I look in through the bars he looks back dismally, when he isn't curled up on his bunk facing away.

The thought kept occurring to me that if he let go much more than he was letting go already, I'd stick my head in his drum one day and find him totally disassembled, arms legs head everything just dropped off for lack of the strength or interest to hold them in place. I said that to him this morning during clean-up while the drums were unlocked. He looked at me for a long moment, almost quizzically, as if he were checking to see if there was anything he really had missed before, then twisted his lips in a half-listless, half-annoyed way and said very distinctly:

---

*A man being charged as an habitual criminal; such charges often carry an open-ended, indefinite sentence.

"It's only important if it's important, ya little dink. When it's not important no more, it's not important. Never really was, mattera fact. So you can go fuck yourself any time."

FRAGMENT

8

At eleven o'clock each evening they turn out the lights and the prison quietens; six hundred men in cages stacked five stories high, the fronts all facing south. No one can see any other, but any guard facing north can see into every cell.

Each man arranges his bedding (two army blankets, a pillow, a sheet), takes a final piss at his tiny toilet and subsides onto his cot. The muttering stops completely. A tiny orange bulb outside my cell backlights the bars, the wire and the guard's catwalk; for the first few nights I tried reading by that light but it was too dim.

Half an hour later the dreams begin, and the submerged, liquid cries. All around me men reopen old battles, unhealed wounds, irrational ecstasies, endless unanswerable questions, arguments drunken and circular, all surfacing erratically in torn underwater gurgles. Ever since my arrival here I have lain wide awake in my cot at this hour, totally fascinated by this shredded drama, trying here or there to reconstruct histories from the bits of debris floated up for brief moments, or listening from farther away to the strange music made by the

26

gropings and stumblings of so many sightless men.

In the next cell down the tier someone gums a fast, mumbling crescendo; that would be the Portuguese brought in on a manslaughter charge and some strange count of having "wilfully been in the place where he was"—I never got that straight. Somewhere below me: "You bitch! an' there wasn't even!" A hoarse muffled yelp, then a scratchy "Dummy the fuck up!" Somewhere above me someone seems to be whining a thin, tuneless lilt, small phrases of song that eventually end as if crushed in the throat. I can hear the guard's boots dragging along the tier up there . . .

FRAGMENT

A dream while in Oakalla:

I stand on a spot I have forgotten, watching a small far-away cluster of projectiles float slowly through the air toward me; I am intrigued, not worried; they approach so slowly, I have plenty of time to move, to step out of their path; I watch with growing fascination, note details, the bright brass and silver casings, tiny starbursts of sunlight slowly unfolding like metal sunflowers in their wakes, the dull pitted lead cones of their tips gently splitting wavery air as they come . . .

Then they are closer, it is time to step aside; the horror of finding out I cannot, that I am in the same slow-motion time warp; my most strenuous efforts to dodge, to get away, slow as gluey toffee, and I can see the bullets floating closer, inexorably accurate and unstoppable; then the slow agonizingly leisurely explosion, my head distintegrating molecules separating the hiss and pop of fissioning cells and all, all fading to water . . .

FRAGMENT

10

It took, I was bemused to note, an astonishingly short time to become a reasonably seasoned jailbird. In no time at all I had learned the language, the prison terminology, the basic assumptions and the basic rules. As soon as possible, I was told, I'd have to make myself a shiv, an old razor blade slotted into a toothbrush handle which becomes an all-purpose tool useful for anything from opening letters to opening throats. If I didn't want to shake it rough I'd have to get myself a racket that would give me bargaining power. The most important thing was to become "solid," to maneuver myself into a position that would provide a dependable defense against whatever difficulties might come up.

Applying all this was a slightly more complex matter, of course, but the school was a rough one and rarely permitted mistakes, so the incentive was there to learn and learn fast. The first thing you needed was allies, and that as quickly as possible. The procedure tended to begin as soon as you were taken from court to the precinct jail, where they gathered the sentenced offenders and handcuffed them two by two for transport to maximum security. You sized up the guy you were handcuffed to and let your instincts do the rest; if he looked like a useful sort, you started up a conversation and established a rapport. You kept this procedure up until you knew enough people to generally cover the territory you were going to run in (e.g., your tier, the exercise yard, your place of work, the gym) and then you chose your friends and chose them carefully, keeping in mind that anything they were involved in would inescapably involve you too. Most of these maneuverings didn't happen quite as mechanically as this may sound, but the rationale behind them was unavoidably clear and few could afford to ignore the routine. A loner or loser in prison was a goner more often than not.

What was always tricky in all this was the business of getting the proportions right. Unless you were a natural ringleader, you wanted on the one hand to maintain your individuality, on the other to keep your profile low enough to avoid attracting unnecessary attention, from both guards and inmates alike. Attention attracted hassle, and too much attention brought on challenges and involvement in power struggles that could be ruinous for anyone dancing between the poised wrecking balls of Administration and the inmate body; unless you were intentionally building an Inside racket you stayed clear of both. As a newcomer, in particular, you adjusted your language to the lowest common denominator, generally refrained from undue shouting and wore your prison clothes as they had been issued, at least for the first while. Meanwhile, you kept alert and absorbed as much information as you could for future reference.

To clarify the remark about prison clothes: it was not uncommon for inmates to alter the cut or tear away pieces of the pants and shirts which were standard prison clothing issue. Again, the trick was to keep the proportions right. A certain amount of alteration might pass as simply an attempt to

30

avoid total submersion in the masses; most, for example, tore up their pantlegs along the seams about half a foot, imitating in some fashion the bell-bottom trouser-leg style. Tearing the arms off a shirt or jacket to create a vest, however, was definitely seen as swaggering and invariably drew challenges when first worn. As in all other matters, you had to earn, to fight for, every unusual possession or characteristic you wanted to maintain, and you were allowed to keep only what you could afford. For a fish (newcomer) to cut down his hard hat into the racy-looking version the "senior" inmates wore (at Stave Lake Prison logging camp), for example, would have been preposterous, not to mention extremely unwise.

In all cases, you had to be able to fight (or its equivalent) your way up to the level you were imitating, and to maintain your position once you got there. In this respect the clothes a person wore in prison were a far more accurate reflection of his accomplishments than a person's clothing Outside, and this made it much easier to "read" a person at a single glance; virtually everything you owned or said or wore was directly symbolic of who you were (or wanted to be).

FRAGMENT

11

It seemed, at first, while I was watching mostly myself and not others, that my good days and bad days had their source demonstrably inside me. When I felt depressed (or not), I could always find in myself a perfectly good reason for these feelings.

But in time I began to notice that when I mentioned my moods to others, they almost always felt the same way, and when I felt miserable, the pall apparently hovering over the entire cell block wasn't simply a projection of my own depression. After I'd grown more accustomed to being Inside and had gotten to know a much larger number of inmates, I found that to an astonishing extent the prison population's feelings moved and changed in unison; a bad day for one tended to be a bad day for all. And this did not appear to be the result of any one inmate taking his cue from another. Something of which all inmates had become a part, some common nervous system into which we had all become plugged, appeared to affect us all more or less at the same time. We had, in some way, effectively become a primitive tribe, with all the intuitive fusion that such community implies, and we could no longer entirely escape from one another even if we hated each other's guts and lived at opposite ends of the tier.

12

They call it the Prison Waltz or the Slammer Shuffle. It's that particular prison walk which is unique to inmates who have done medium- or maximum-security time and is like no other walk I've ever seen. It's different primarily because its purpose differs from that of a walk along an open street; the shuffle isn't intended to get anyone anywhere; it's the walk of a man going noplace. At the same time it's designed to cover a large distance, tirelessly, like the pacing of a caged animal—because that's essentially what it is.

Since pacing implies a troubled state of mind, the Shuffle has other characteristics built into it as well. It's not a good thing to be visibly troubled in prison; immediate assumptions are made about one's stability, about the chances that one might be planning an escape, about one's "not adapting well into the program," etc. So the Shuffle tends to make a man in some way diminutive, in some obscure fashion nonvisible, somehow almost nonexistent. Head down and weaving slightly, eyes focused inward and arms crossed behind his back, the shuffler paces from wall to wall or gate to gate like a mechanical toy, deep in thought or functionally mindless, lost in some underwater labyrinth of his own. But since a man deep in thought might be surprised in this place, which is by definition full of the unexpected, the shuffler walks instinctively on the forward part of the foot, rocking from instep to toes, thus constantly alert in body if not in mind. I've seen prisoners walk for hours and hours in this way.

Walking in prison actually covers many of the same functions as drinking does on the Outside; where a man on the Street might invite a friend to join him in a cup of coffee or a beer, an inmate suggests: "Wanna walk a bit?" Often two, three or even four inmates get up to walk together, and the result might reasonably be compared to the performance of a well-synchronized chorus line. In a neat even row, their paces measured and matched, deep in conversation, the walkers stride along until they arrive at the opposite wall or barrier, where, still in perfect unison, without the slightest break in rhythm or conversation, they whirl neatly about, right foot swinging forward, left up and then down and they're off again, still in perfect unison and heading for the opposite wall, where they'll turn again and come back. This, too, I have seen continue for hours, and nobody missing a step.

13

Roster left a few days ago; they transferred him to the penetentiary across town. He'd been in here awaiting the results of an appeal and had lost it. They took him away without warning, on Thursday, while we were out in the exercise yard. When I came back there was another man sitting on Rosco's bunk, unpacking a paper bag.

"Howdy. Where's Rosco?"

"The guy was here before me? Off to the pen, I guess. Scored a few extra years when he blew his appeal. Actually, I knew him pretty good, old Rosco."

"No shit."

"Yeah. Used to live in Coquitlam close to the Continental Bar. Used to get in some great brawls in there. Used to drop 'em like flies in there."

"Coquitlam. Jesus. You wouldn't by any chance be Hazler, or Hatler or something like that . . ."

"Hartling. Yeah, that's me. What, old Rosco tell you about me?"

"As a matter of fact, he mentioned you a couple of times.

It was when you mentioned the Continental Bar that I clicked."

"Yeah, we dropped a few of them in there all right. Great bar, that place. Used to drop 'em with turned-over chairs, tables, anything. Old Rosco was all right, actually."

His name is Barry, he's about thirty-thirty-five and he's a little weird. He's a body-building fanatic, spends every available moment in the gym and the rest of the time in the kitchen trying to get the cooks to "give me some greens." Since we don't get salads in here all that often his chances should be fairly slim, but he manages somehow anyway, and now the back of his mattress where he's slit it open and removed the stuffing is full of lettuce and cabbage leaves, carrots and the occasional stalk of rhubarb. He nibbles on the stuff every chance he gets, day or night, and I've become accustomed to falling asleep to the sounds of munching and gnawing above me as if there were a giant rabbit up there. Last night, just as I was dropping off to sleep:

"Hey, Schroeder."

"Mmphff."

"Hey, Schroeder, getta loada these beans. Casey give 'em to me yesterday in the laundry." A hand clutching a fistful of beans descended from above. "Have some."

"Aw fuck off, Barry; I'm trying to shut off my head."

The hand with the beans dropped a little lower. "No really, kid, ya oughta eat more of this stuff. Great for the muscle tone. Drop anybody if ya chew on these every day. Drop any cocksucker who gets in your way. Ever actually drop anybody?"

"Only my wallet and the occasional dime in a phone booth." It was pointless trying to sleep when Barry was in a conversational mood. "Here, gimme a few of those." I pulled three beans from between the fingers and the hand rose back up and disappeared. "Hey, Barry."

37

"Yeah?"

"How'd you get into this stuff about dropping people all the time?"

There was a pause.

"Whaddya mean?"

"Well, you know, this preoccupation you have with beating people's brains out."

Another pause.

"Why d'ya wanna know for?"

"Just interested. You talk about it all the time."

Pause. Barry's face dropped over the side of the bunk. He stared at me carefully. "Ya sound like a shrink."

"Okay. Let's pretend I am one. Feel like playing that game?"

"Why?"

"Do you *know* why you keep beating on people?"

"Cause they keep gettin in my way. That's why."

"How come people don't seem to get in *my* way all the time? How come they always seem to get only in yours?"

Barry thought that one over for a while. Then he looked at me impishly and grinned. "Cause you're just a little bugger."

"Aw fuck off. Really, tell me why."

He stared at me again for a while, his face becoming just a shade darker and a trifle uneasy. "You tryin to tell me I'm nuts?"

"Hey, come off it, Barry; I'm not laying any shit on you. If you don't want to play you don't have to. I've just been hearing you talk about it so long, I get to wondering, is all. If it bugs you, forget it. I'd really rather sleep anyway."

But he was interested now, and thoughtful. He pulled a bean apart into its segments, chewing them one by one. He looked at me again, craftily. "You figure you could tell me what a shrink'd say?"

I thought that one over myself. "You *want* to know what a shrink would say?"

38

"Ah yeah, sort of."

I sat back on my bunk and ate the last bean. "Well, I'm certainly no shrink but I guess I've got an idea as to the sort of things they'd ask. You want to know the sort of thing they'd ask?"

"They already asked me stuff."

"Oh yeah? You've been to see the shrinks already? They ask you about your family?"

"Yup."

"They ask you about your dad?"

"Yup."

"Your dad beat you up a lot?"

Barry's face held for a moment, then disappeared back over the edge and his feet swung down. He stepped to the toilet and took a piss, then sat down on the far end of my bunk. His face looked slightly annoyed or troubled. "How come you askin all these questions?"

"*You* wanted to know about what a shrink would ask. It was your idea."

"Well, yeah, I guess so. But I mean, well, yeah, I guess my old man was a real sonofabitch."

"Did you ever hit him back?"

Barry's face glowed briefly. "Not until about three years ago. Then I dropped him good one night. Left home after that too." He smacked a clenched fist into a cupped one appreciatively. "Boy could he ever rumble, though. Boy he was good!"

"D'you ever see him now?"

"Oh sure. Sometimes."

"You do?"

"Sure."

"And you get along with him all right?"

"Oh yeah. Pretty well."

I looked at him hard to see if he was bluffing. "So why are you still knocking people around?"

"Whaddya mean?"

39

"I mean, if you're getting along with your dad all right, how come you still beat people over the head?"

Barry looked at me forcefully, a clear probing look. "Are you sayin I drop people cause I been havin all this trouble with my old man?"

"Yeah, I guess that's what I'm suggesting."

He looked at me for a little longer in the same way, then broke into a wide grin, stood up and clapped me good-humoredly on the shoulder.

"Jesus, I bet you'd be a blast to get stoned with," he said.

Then climbed up to his bunk and went to sleep.

FRAGMENT

14

When I came in from the exercise yard today Barry was waiting outside our cell, gesticulating urgently.

"Quick, man, the Indian's gone bananas!"

I threw my coat across my bunk and we ducked into the next cell where the Indian lived. He was sitting on his bunk, legs folded underneath him, arms under his knees and his face a strange bluish brown. His eyes were closed and he was rocking slightly, talking to himself comfortingly in a small sing-song voice as he swayed:

"She calling, she calling. Yeah, she calling. Gonna have to go. Comin pretty soon, comin right now. Have to go to her right away; she calling. Yeah, I can hear her; gotta go now, time to go. Yeah, she calling, she calling."

He rocked some more and then opened his eyes and saw us there, blocking the door to his drum. He looked us over briefly but the look was faraway and I don't think he knew we were there; he paused for a moment as if listening, then slowly crawled off his bunk. "Gotta go now," he explained tonelessly, to no one in particular. "Time to go; she calling."

41

"What's he doin?" Barry whispered.

Before I could answer there was a sudden series of metallic clashes like a long freight train being jerked into motion, and the doors to all the cells along the tier began to close.

"Jesus, lock-up!" Barry swore, scrambling past me into the corridor. "Get outta there pronto, man, or you'll be locked in with that turkey!"

We skidded into our drum just barely in time, the door almost catching my hand. I stood at the bars, listening in the direction of the Indian's cell.

"Can ya hear anythin?"

I couldn't hear anything at all. Then suddenly I could. A coughing, spluttering sound.

"Hey, Schroeder!" That was Bartowitz in number fourteen.

"What?"

"What's going on in seventeen?"

I wanted to be sure. "Why?"

"Buncha gurgling 'n stuff comin from in there."

"Yeah, I'm hearing the same thing. I think he's doing himself in."

"Think we should call the bulls?"

I was in a serious quandary. I'd been listening to him for three nights already and I felt I had an idea about what was going on in his head. Somehow, despite all my rational inclinations, I couldn't quite convince myself that I had a right to interfere: he was working out his own salvation for his own reasons; didn't he have the right to his own solutions?

The steady rattling of bars solved the dilemma at least for the moment; a bull was coming up the tier, testing the doors as he came.

"Screw's already coming, Bartowitz. Guess he'll check it out."

The rattling came closer, then suddenly the guard stood before me through the bars.

"Better check seventeen pretty carefully on your way through."

He gave the bars of our door a thorough tug and peered into the drum.

"How come?"

"Indian's choking in there, sounds like."

"Oh yeah?"

He took several steps toward number seventeen and I heard him tugging at the Indian's door. There was a brief pause. I could still hear the sounds.

"What the he . . ."

I heard his key chain clatter and the manual override key clank into the lock and then the door scraping open.

"Hey! Get outta there! Come on!"

The sound of a body thudding on concrete, then the guard's quick footsteps. He flashed by our bars and down the tier, moving rapidly.

"Hey, Schroeder."

"What?"

"Think he caught it?"

"Can't tell."

The guard returned with two others and a stretcher. There was muffled activity in the cell for some minutes, then all reappeared, the Indian's body stretched on the canvas. I couldn't see whether he was alive or dead.

"What's going on?"

". . . his head in the toilet, the old bastard. Naw, he'll live. Guess he'll do a little psych-time for a while . . ."

The entourage passed on down the tier, fading out of earshot.

"Hey, Schroeder."

"What?"

"Did he catch it?"

"Nope."

Pause.

"Fuck eh?"

"Yeah."

FRAGMENT

15

The terms *prison* and *homosexuality* are almost always
linked in people's minds, and I must admit I was a bit nervous
about the possible connection myself. Now I'm Inside, however, I find that it's mostly another story; true, there's a lot of
talk about it and much suggestive insinuation, but I have yet
to see an actual sexual attack. By the second day I found
out that if you want to get yourself tangled up in homosexual
matters, you hang around in a poorly lit tunnel which connects the West Wing cell block with the laundry complex. If
you have no such inclinations, you stay out of there. In
matters of sexual assault, that's the first line of defense.

The second, as in all other matters, is to maintain a sufficient number of allies. As long as you keep your contacts and
alliances up, you can keep almost any prison trouble at bay.
Invariably, it is the man who tries to go it on his own or who
for some reason has been labeled undesirable who becomes
the statistic everyone hears about.* Such men are quickly

*Several months before I entered Oakalla they did have a serious case of
sexual attack at the Haney Correctional Centre, just up the valley. During

pushed to one side and often end up drifting about on the periphery, an easy target for anyone looking for someone to harass without having to worry about half a dozen cohorts promptly pouring out of the woodwork. I suppose it stands to reason that such men are also the obvious candidates for enforced homosexual "marriages," although I haven't yet seen one. No doubt they do exist, but the point is that there's obviously much less flagrant homosexual coercion Inside than the movies or the dime novelists would have us believe.

I must emphasize, however, that I've been speaking only about *enforced* homosexual activity; there is always, assuredly, a certain amount of open, voluntary homosexuality going on, but that is quite another matter. For one thing, there are the "queens," the transvestites or the trans-sexuals who have often undergone partial or even major sex-change operations but who are still sentenced to, and generally confined in, all-male prisons. I must confess I was thoroughly taken aback at my first view of a row of male prisoners and queens, who, having just arrived from the courts, were filing into the Records Office. Some, to be sure, were pathetic beyond belief, but some were nothing of the sort at all; with richly upswept hair, clinging gowns and often remarkably full breasts, graceful figures and a thoroughly feminine bearing, they were astonishingly beautiful and they knew it. "Ain't that a sight?" an inmate standing near me chuckled, amused at my astonished stare. "To tell the truth, I still get a mite surprised every time myself."

---

the night, six men in a cell block dormitory fitted socks under the edges of three portable sets of lockers to muffle the sound, then slid them across the room and around the bed of a young loser whom they suspected (or *said* they suspected) of being a stoolpigeon. While four inmates alternated in holding him down, the rest gang-raped him "through the fleet" until all six had violated him several times. "Little fucker kept squealing like a stuck pig," one of the "noninvolved" inmates of the dormitory (who was doing a subsequent stretch in Oakalla on our tier) told us. "But he sure as hell won't rat on nobody no more."

45

The queens tend to find it somewhat less than difficult to find willing lovers, and one also hears occasionally of straight male homosexual love affairs, which are voluntary and don't impose on anyone. The guards seem ambivalent about the whole issue; they'll break it up if they catch two men in bed, but they'll ignore whatever they only hear about, provided that it's discreet and isn't causing any trouble. The doctor supplies the queens with hormone medication to keep their breasts from collapsing and their hair from growing back (the same medication regular Street doctors give them Outside), and they're given extra protection if they need it. The only thing they're not allowed to do once they're Inside is wear a dress.

FRAGMENT

16

The day before yesterday, about three weeks after I entered Oakalla, I was finally classified and informed I'd be sent to Stave Lake Prison Camp, a first-offenders' institution situated deep in the bush well north of Haney, B.C. Several others on my tier were assigned to the same place, and most of the rest were classified to the Haney Correctional Centre, which also houses the operational offices for a satellite system of prison camps (of which Stave Lake is one) scattered about the area. The transfer route was to be Haney Correctional (a short stop to off-load those prisoners consigned to that place), then on to Stave Lake Camp which, I was assured, we'd reach by nightfall.

It's evening now and I'm sitting here in a cell in Haney Correctional's House Five cell block, cold, depressed and pissed off. Stave Lake, it appears, is full to capacity and the next man being released out of there won't be leaving for over two weeks. We'll have to wait it out in here, they say, or possibly in a nearby prison camp called Pine Ridge. I don't know about Pine Ridge, but this prison is bad news. It's incredibly noisy, ugly and dirty, full of teen-age hoodlums and thugs, and the guards seem to blow up at the slightest provocation, of which there are many. When it turned out we wouldn't be going on to Stave Lake we had to go through the whole fingerprinting, mug-shot and fill-in-the-forms routine again, and then they rounded us up and shaved most of our hair off (for "sanitary reasons"). For a while there, I thought I was going to see my first prison riot from a ringside seat.

This morning, at Oakalla, it was even worse. They herded us into a long, exceptionally narrow, windowless room fitted with wooden benches, to await our departure. After the usual interminable delays we were marched through various corridors, stairwells and tunnels out across the yard and into two waiting prison vans, where they removed our handcuffs. The doors crashed shut, the long curtains of steel meshing inside the truck (between the cab's rear window and us) began their clatter in synch with the engine, there was torn and shredded foam-rubber upholstery all over the floor and everyone collided with everyone else as the truck lunged off. By the time we'd sorted ourselves out and renegotiated places to sit, the guards had stopped laughing in the cab up front and the one not driving had settled his eyes against the peephole to the back. It was agreed that running a red-hot poker through those eyeballs would do for a start.

Then I heard the word "skinner" for the first time in my life. Somebody said we had us a skinner in the back of the truck.

I inadvertently interrupted the sudden silence this remark occasioned by being overheard asking the man on my right what a skinner was; I'd always thought a skinner drove a cat. That was greeted with howls of laughter and a lot of suggestive commentary, and then they turned back to the business at hand: a thin, frightened-looking eighteen-year-old kid who, I was told, had been charged and sentenced for indecent assault.

48

It started very quickly; a man I hadn't particularly noticed before had already left his seat and was shouldering his way toward the kid; his back at first obscured my view of both faces.

"You a skinner, kid?"

Silence.

Whack! "Asked if you was a skinner, kid."

Muffled reply.

Whack! "Speak up, you mangy little fucker!" *Whack!* "Huh? Shout it out loud and clear, there; whaddya do? Eh? Fuck a kid? Eh?" *Whack!* "Slimy little turd; whaddya fuck, eh?" *Whack!* "Come on, spit it out; did ya screw babies, eh?" *Whack! Whack! WHACK! !*

The last blow knocked the kid clean across the back of the truck, his face suddenly visible again. Blood was pouring from his nose and the skin was broken across one cheekbone. The man he fell against brought up his knee and rammed it into the kid's groin, reversing his direction; his receiver repeated the block and deflected him into a waiting fist on the other side. The beating continued for what was probably only minutes but seemed like half an hour, and the guard's eyes never left the peephole.

When we arrived at Haney the security staff took the kid into protective custody, where they threw him into the Hole. The guy who ring-leadered the beating drew ten days there himself, and a lot of glory. The kid disappeared after that, rumor having it that they'd caged him for good, now that he was branded both a skinner and a rat. You can't live among a regular prison population with the reputation of being a rat; fatal accidents happen to such people, and everybody knows it.

*　　　*　　　*

The incident with the skinner shook me up a good deal; I'd never heard of that particular ritual before and I was totally unprepared for it. I realized, from the immediate understanding that had united most of the other inmates in the truck at the word "skinner" and from the prompt, unrestrained beating, that I had stumbled onto a tradition, a well-entrenched convention. I think what confused me most was the affectation of moral outrage that seemed to underlie the custom. I couldn't understand why that particular offense should be considered so much more heinous than any other, particularly by inmates many of whom were doing time for a wide variety of violent crimes. While we were waiting in a holding cell I asked an inmate seated next to me what it was all about. The question seemed to put him somewhat on the defensive; he said: "Well, we got wives an' daughters an' girl friends out there on the Street, man. You let these fuckers get away with this sort of shit, there ain't goin to be any safety out there for 'em. Guys in here'll have to worry all the time. You just gotta make sure these skinners get that idea outta their heads, see what I mean?"

I didn't see what he meant; it just didn't make any sense. I asked a few more inmates and got largely the same answers; it seemed like a party line and nobody seemed overly anxious to investigate it. And now I think I know what it's all about. Possibly without even really realizing it, the prison population has created for itself a Judas goat, a method of passing on the pain, the anger, the outrage. A primitive sort of lightning rod, if you will. In his castigation of the skinner the convict proposes to establish that he hasn't yet sunk to the very bottom; that as long as he remains in a position to denounce another man's sins, he is by implication superior to that man.

The castigation, in fact, becomes in all its implications a grotesque parody of what has happened to a convict himself, who of course has been similarly misunderstood. And I don't mean this facetiously either; I have never yet met a person (convict or otherwise) who, having been dealt the short end of the stick, felt he deserved precisely what he received in

50

exactly the way he received it. The next man, of course, generally appears to deserve much more (often all) of what he gets, and so the misapplication of justice in other people's lives is rarely as self-evident as it is in one's own . . .

In the holding cell at Haney; the rumor has just floated in
that they're going to cut our hair. Instant tumult. "Those
fuckin bastards as much as touch my head . . ." "My civil
rights, man! That's violatin my civil rights!" Most of us have
long hair, many have beards. Haney Correctional officials appear not to be overly interested in civil rights; the guards open
the cage and one of them reads from a list of names.

"Hartfield! Front and center!"

An Afro-haired (more or less) lanky man disentangles himself from the group but does not approach the door.

"Whaddya want?"

"Up to the barber shop. Hustle!"

"Ain't goin to no barber shop."

"You'd rather do a bit of solitary?"

"Fuck you."

The Afro-haired man steps back to the corner of the cell
and sits down.

The guard lays the list of names aside carefully.

"You coming to the barber shop or not?"

"Fuck you."

The guards move in practiced unison, quickly. It sounds like seals snorting, the body flopping, that adrenalin-producing sound of men panting in combat. The Afro-haired man makes no sound. He writhes and struggles grimly, making it as difficult as possible, contorting and wrenching in their grasp. They maneuver him deftly to the door, twist him through and shut it with a crash. All three disappear down the corridor, the sound of the Afro-haired man's dragging feet fading like a slowly exhaling breath.

"Those goddamn bas . . ." someone behind me starts, then stops. The cell is clenched with white and flushed faces.

The barber shop has four chairs and a series of seats along one wall. We file in and sit on the benches, watching the student barbers at work. The Haney Correctional Centre is proud of its barbers, we're told. Haney inmates receive a haircut a week.

As the chairs become free, the guards nudge new inmates to occupy them. One after another we settle into the plastic cushions. The barbers work methodically, their faces expressionless. The hair drops from the shears in great tufts, often ankle-deep around the chairs before an apprentice sweeps it away. The seats against the wall slowly begin to fill with strangers, new, angry, naked-looking faces, averted eyes, oddly embarrassed, humiliated looks.

As the clippers buzz across my head I feel a hot surge of resentment flush my cheeks. It's true, there's something mysterious about this act; it's like being violated in some deeply outrageous way and I can feel my stomach and face muscles go rigid with resentment, despite the fact that I know it's dangerous. One of the things I have already learned in prison is never to let them get to you, never to let them know exactly where you live; that is your only advantage, your only edge. Without that your situation is always potentially out of control; without that, anybody can push any of your buttons and watch you self-destruct for the sheer entertainment of it. The minute it's discovered that you have anything to lose they're on you like sharks, and your foolish thrashing to defend your little bauble simply guarantees your defeat. And once you're wounded, you're lost; prison is no place to convalesce.

The clippers chatter down my cheeks and across my chin. Sideburns and beard curl across the barber's hand and drop in four thick swaths onto my lap. I stare across the room into the mirror on the opposite wall and see a foolish, astonished fifteen-year-old kid staring back.

We don't know what to do. It's becoming precarious, that much is certain; it has to be taken in hand. Somebody starts to laugh, loud, high-pitched horse laughter, and then we all join in, snorting and jeering, pointing at each other and describing what we see in the most derisive manner possible. If we have no choice but to submit to this outrage, we're at least going to make it our own. "Hey, Harry, you can be my boy any time!" "Go shave your balls, Gloria; you can be the baby of this happy family!" "Geez, Corse, you look like you're only half the man you used to be; better take off your pants and find out!"

The guards begin to look uncomfortable and assume belligerent expressions; one of the barbers hesitates for a moment, then continues cutting away Greg's sideburns. "Smooth as a baby's ass," he misunderstands hopefully, running his fingers along the shaven cheek. Greg's face freezes for a moment, then relaxes and he half-turns in the chair. "You won't live long with a yap like that," he says almost pleasantly, then slams the back of his hand across the barber's face so that his glasses shoot from his nose and his clippers fly in a neat arch across the room. Somebody steps on the clippers where they lie on the floor, breaking the black plastic housing. "Awfully sorry," he says, handing them back. "Couldn't see them properly for the dark."

And that's as far as it goes, though it doesn't feel nearly enough. Greg is frog-marched off to solitary and the rest of us lapse back into silence. For the next several days we keep checking our reflections furtively in windowpanes and shiny surfaces, trying to arrange what little remains of our hair to appear as bushy as possible. Requests for outside visits for the next few weeks are about as hot an item as applications for psychiatric examinations and requests for isolation cells.

FRAGMENT

18

A dream while in Haney Correctional Centre.

Main scene: an underground, tunneled and many-tiered maze of cages; people happily crying, ecstatic, intoxicated with joy busily arranging themselves inside. As the cages fill, amid happy cries, the doors clang shut; faces, arms and legs come through the bars encouraging us to hurry, to lock ourselves in before it is too late. I and one other run through the tunnels looking for someone; we can't find the person anywhere and time is getting short. The calls and encouragement are breaking down my companion's defenses; I can feel him weakening. Finally we begin to pass a cage that still has three vacant seats—the occupants solicit with frenzied shouts, lunges, exhortations, passionate revivalist fervor, and my companion, face fiercely contorted with inner struggle, suddenly breaks and staggers into the cage.

Instantly, having made the decision, he becomes one of them, stretching his hands toward me with hopeful and beckoning cries, trying his best to induce me to take the second seat (and whom is the third seat for?). I feel myself running in all directions inside me, this way and that, then finally with a great shout breaking away and running, running, past all the gesticulating frenzied hands through the bars, bars, bars . . .

And just as they're closing the front gates I burst through (the wire rips part of my sleeve, tears at my arm) and am on the street, the evening blinking a deep royal blue through beckoning neon. I stagger up the street, the image of the cages slowly melting in my head, a flood of relief beginning from far back inside me, washing over me in a warm, glowing surge . . .

Sometimes I think there is only one way to pass unscathed through this maze of tunnels and cages:

To navigate with one's entire nervous system unhooked.

FRAGMENT

20

Part of the strain of being in prison is the continual fear of feeling bad, the constant sitting under that trembling drop of poison which, if shaken loose, will spread slowly but inexorably like a stain on wet paper through your life, unstoppable, disastrous. Because you know you *have* to stay healthy in this place. The only defense against the undertow that keeps people here half their lives is never to forget that you *want* to get out, that the present is transitory and must be kept in transit, that it is therefore necessary to resist the urge to take offense, to escape, to revolt or fight back, which would simply subtract what you've already put behind you and start the wheel rolling from the beginning again. All around you you see men letting go and closing the vicious circle, men escaping for a single night with their wives, men plotting revenge that will only double their prison terms, men swaggering in defiance of a machine that isn't paying the slightest attention, its meter simply adding the years, implacably.

And so you sit in constant guard duty on yourself, watching carefully for any signs of approaching depression, of the beginnings of hatred or bitterness, and if you feel them coming, feel the possibility develop, you bring your most massive defenses to bear, any twisted or absurd forms of logic, stern talkings-to in your corner to yourself, the company of another inmate who is just then riding high and can afford to clap you on the shoulder. You plunder your little store of medicine or magic, a letter that put you in a good mood last time, memories you normally only unwrap at night, a carefully saved-up smuggled-in cigar, anything; whatever will deflect or snap the mood.

Occasionally, fortunately, there are those times when you can see far enough ahead to line up predictably "good" events, and if there are enough of them to keep your life safely afloat for a week or two, you can allow yourself a few hours or even evenings of glorious despondency. This becomes, of course, a carefully monitored depression, with all sorts of special safeguards immediately in the wings in case you begin to take yourself too seriously. But for a few pleasant hours you can then give your real feelings free play, feel rotten as hell, hate the bastards up one side and down the other, gripe and bitch and snarl—which, if nothing else, feels at least a little more honest, since you know that's probably how you'd feel most of the time if you could afford it.

FRAGMENT

Of the prisons I've come to know, Haney Correctional Centre is unquestionably the worst. This prison seems to me, for all intents and purposes, largely out of control, and I don't see how it can go on this way much longer.

Certainly it has the nature of its inmate population to contend with, which is a difficult proposition at best. Very roughly speaking, H.C.C. is the juvenile equivalent of Oakalla, a maximum security institution for younger men (approximately eighteen to thirty) who are for the most part repeaters, chronic offenders, longer-term graduates of juvenile detention homes and institutions. Where Oakalla's inmate body has a complement of older men to stabilize it, Haney is full of confused, swaggering hoodlums; where Oakalla's inmates keep rigorously to themselves, often ordering their affairs discreetly (if a trifle violently) on their own with as little reference to security and administrative personnel as possible, H.C.C. is thoroughly infiltrated with rats and informers; denunciations occur regularly and the level of suspicion, subterfuge and just plain dirty pool is nothing if not disastrous.

There is, in short, no firm and long-standing tradition to settle the prison down, and as anyone connected with prisons (inmate or staff) can tell you, there is no rest in such a place. The prison staff is as quickly and hopelessly drawn into the maelstrom as the inmates, and in the resulting melee everybody loses. I've never seen so many blinded human beings flailing away at each other in darkened rooms as I've seen at H.C.C., and yet that's where most of the "rehabilitation programs" are carried out.

The first thing that hit me was the noise. Even at its most unrestrained, Oakalla never sounded this loud. Over a steady backdrop of clashing steel doors and shrilling hinges there is incessant shouting, arguing, irritated commands; a constant back-and-forth stream of inmates ("trainees" they call them here) pouring through the corridors, harassed trainers snapping at their heels or, already quite demoralized, marching tiredly at their head, oblivious to the horseplay behind. Small tight knots of inmates keep exploding into fights in the dining hall, the cell blocks and the stairwells and corridors, and the tiled facing on some of the floors and walls deflects the sound into two directions at once, effectively doubling the noise level with the echo. The thought once struck me, as I was sitting in a holding cage watching the tumult convulsing by, that the whole thing was really like a B-grade psychological western, inasmuch as everybody seemed to be constantly firing off their sawed-off nerve endings at each other.

But the most irritating thing in this prison is that something is constantly being *done* to you; you're continually being interviewed, tested, programmed, questioned, assessed, examined, transferred, reprogrammed, re-examined, retested and reclassified. It seems to do little good. The inmates remain querulous and uncooperative, and during the last few weeks alone two major riots have torn a good piece of the prison apart, breaking every single window in two complete cell blocks (approximately two hundred panes) and leaving

62

behind an almost ineradicable stench of burned mattresses, fried plastic and charred clothes. One inmate was taken to hospital with a length of lead pipe buried in his skull and a second was just about to be hanged in his own cell by his enemies when the guards burst through the barricades with water hoses. After a thorough dousing of everything and everyone, the inmates were locked into their cells for two days, sitting on their soaked bunks in their sopping clothes, shivering. No one, to the best of my knowledge, was ever brought to outside court on the matter, although I gather some "loose ends" are still being investigated. (Since the whole debacle happened in House One and Two cell blocks, and the rest of the prison was immediately quarantined, the word only filtered through in rumors and I didn't even see the smashed windows from the outside until almost a week later.)

Nor do the guards have an easy time of it in Haney. They're underpaid and underexperienced; most of them are simply filling in time while searching for better jobs, and so their one objective tends always to be to simply get out of there as quickly as possible each day and to hell with it; let the place blow apart as long as they aren't close enough to stop a knife or a bullet. One can hardly blame them, of course, but on the other hand they are the final x-factor in the equation, and the combination of unruly inmates and embittered guards is a deadly mixture.

What has become particularly tricky is that I suspect things have developed to such a stage that no one can really *afford* to be sensible any longer; the battle lines have been drawn (by someone; probably no one even knows who anymore) and each man is now obliged to stick to his own kind for his own safety. All the willingness in the world seems no longer able to induce any man to risk his neck to try to re-establish communication with the other side, especially if he is an inmate. Only the natural leaders of either side can afford such an attempt, and they don't seem overly anxious to try. It's a bad stalemate state of affairs, and I wouldn't be surprised if it comes to a bad and bloody end one of these days.*

---

*It didn't, at least not bad and bloody. The Haney Correctional Centre was formally phased out of the B.C. prison system in early fall of 1975. At last report, they've turned the place into a juvenile Remand Centre. Most prisons include a remand section, which houses prisoners without bail awaiting trial.

About a dozen of us are being transferred to Pine Ridge Camp. Stave Lake is still closed and Pine Ridge is short of workers; its sawmill operation just outside the perimeter fence of the Haney Correctional Centre is running at half capacity. We're crowded into a small committee room where each of us is interviewed in turn by a tall, brisk man who sports a loud bark and a sharp, harsh manner. It appears that since Pine Ridge is officially classed as a minimum-security establishment, we must all be checked for "propensity to escape."

"Scott!" (Scott moves toward the desk.) "Siddown kid; grab that chair. Okay now, what's your beef?"

"Possession for the purpose."

"Possession, possession; possession of *what*, for chrissake??"

"Oh. Uh, grass."

"Uh-huh. Well, you got any particular plans to pull a little Code Two on us in the next while or so?"

"A Code Two?"

"Escape, for chrissake, escape!"

"Oh. Uh, no."

"Speak up, kid. Any intentions to Code Two?"

"No. No, course not."

"Course not, hell. Well, okay, I guess you'll do. Harris!"

"Yessir."

"Siddown kid, on that chair there. Now then, what's your beef?"

"B and E, sir."

"Handy with the old crowbar, eh? Well, you got any plans to pull a Code Two on us in the next little while?"

"No sir. Definitely not." (Harris is a little guy with wire-rimmed glasses. He says he installs furnaces for a trade.)

"You quite sure about that?"

"Yessir, quite sure."

"Well, we'll try you. Donzella!"

And so it proceeds. When the interviews are over we're all issued size XL jackets, a toothbrush and a razor with blades (the first significant sign that we're really shifting to minimum), then led through barrier after barrier down to Control on the ground floor, where a guard standing at the electric gates checks our names against our photographs and our photographs against us. We're made to stand against the wall in a neat row and then, as our names are called and the officer in Control makes a final double-check of his list, we're searched and released through the gates into the entrance corridor. From there a quick march through an inner court-yard takes us to the Main Gate and a waiting truck.

The camp is only about a quarter-mile away, and we arrive in less than five minutes. Seven green-painted huts lie at even intervals around a horseshoe driveway, surrounded in turn by a series of spotlights mounted on tall poles. The camp doesn't have an overly healthy reputation, but as we stand and look the place over we're almost giddy with relief at being free of the steel and the concrete and that constant tunneled feeling one gets in maximum-security jails. Everybody kids around while we wait for the officers to finish their palaver in the office. Somebody grabs Harris's toothbrush and throws it into bushes about thirty yards beyond the office but Harris just leaves it there.

We stand in a fairly tight group at the front of the truck, still waiting for the officers to come out. Burton and Corso fool around trying to step on each other's shoes while we all watch and make a few comments. Finally the officer in charge comes out and announces that there'll be a brew-up before we're assigned to our huts, and points to the mess hall. Then he re-enters the office.

And that's when I finally realize that something has been bothering me ever since we got here; something is not quite right. Somehow our pleasure has been mixed with a certain unease, a nervousness that suddenly comes to a head when the officer points to the mess hall and disappears; the whole bunch of us mill about purposefully, but nobody makes any decisive moves for at least fifteen seconds before Lukin Jarvis finally strikes out across the grass toward the hall.

And then it hits me; by god, we're already showing the symptoms of the inevitable corral syndrome despite the fact that we've been Inside for only a month: that unthinking plodding along predetermined paths outlined by fences and barriers which totally eliminates the need for making any decisions about where to go and where to stop. Here, under open sky and with no fencing to provide security against making costly mistakes, we're being affected by what amounts to a touch of agoraphobia, an uneasiness about open spaces to which we've become totally unaccustomed. Suddenly we're back in a world that deals in ambiguities, that relies on arbitrary decisions and on faith. In a jail without clear deadlines (wires or demarcations indicating boundaries that may not be overstepped on pain of a guard's bullet), how can you ever tell exactly whether you are in or out? Who wants to take the risk of adjudicating such a question? And whom would you trust with the decision? In the cells, at least, we had always known precisely where we stood, which had removed the need for anybody trusting anyone; here, where the wire is invisible but no less real, there is the constant danger of getting snarled up in it before you even know it's there. There is, after all, some truth to the old adage that the imaginary cage is often the most insidious cage of all.

FRAGMENT

23

One of the first things I discovered when I entered the B.C. penal system was that most of its prisons are swamped by radio. Each cell and/or corridor is fitted with well-grated speakers, very occasionally flanked by a volume control but never by a kill button. We were, in other words, obliged to listen to rock music from 7:00 A.M. to 10:30 P.M., and no place to hide. In Oakalla the situation was even worse in that the bottom tier of cells, generally inhabited by older inmates consigned to do their entire time in maximum security, had the odd television set and private radio as well, so that at any given time we stood a good chance of being attacked by three radio stations, two television soundtracks and the public-address system to boot.

In Oakalla, admittedly, the newness of the whole experience absorbed a good deal of my attention and so the strange tossed salad of sound, considerably hollowed and eeried by the vastness of the building, and by the fact that each bank of speakers transmitted from a different level in the joint (there were five levels of cells), simply confirmed the fantastical

69

nature of the place; it was the macabre soundtrack of some prehistoric time and therefore peculiarly appropriate.

The Haney Correctional Centre's sound system was worse because even the corridors were wired for sound (which echoed badly), but at least they had managed to get themselves plugged into FM programming, which keeps its commercials to a tolerable level. But when I arrived at Pine Ridge Camp I found the whole idea expanded from the ridiculous to the perverse. Not only were the individual huts wired into AM radio, but the entire camp was surrounded by speakers mounted on telephone poles which flooded the camp area morning and night with rock and pop music. (I might add that I used to be fairly fond of rock and pop music before my Pine Ridge sojourn.) We used to remark sourly that you couldn't have heard a bird sing if you'd attached a bullhorn to your ear and aimed it directly at the bird screaming in the tree under which you were standing. And all this not, incidentally, because inmates wanted it that way. I couldn't begin to count the number of times we asked the duty officer to shut the damn thing off, our ears were ringing and some of us wanted to sleep, to read, etc.—all to no avail. The camp staff insisted that we wanted that music, even if for some peculiar reason we didn't realize that we did.

It was that music which finally drove me to the only significant loss of cool to which I ever succumbed in prison. Not that I didn't despair at regular intervals, lose my temper and curse my fate as enthusiastically as the next man—I did, but never to such an extent that I totally lost control of it. Mostly the turmoil just unreeled itself in my head while I kept a wary eye on the fuses, and when it was done, rewound itself politely, its purpose accomplished. This time I had no such luck. It had been a bad day, pouring rain again, torn raingear, no mail, sloppy food and all evening some demented disc jockey on CKLG enthusing all over the place in that ludicrous hip jargon they sometimes affect, with loud, brassy band music hour after hour. I finally suggested we tear the goddamn speaker out of the ceiling.

We considered the proposition seriously for some time but decided, upon investigation, that the speaker was wired in series, meaning that if we unhooked ours, the entire system would fall silent and we'd have a guard at the door in about three micro-seconds flat. I decided to muffle the speaker instead.

That was easier said than done inasmuch as the ceiling was ten feet high and there was nothing to attach anything to up there. I finally concocted an absurd Tower of Babel by jamming a towel-filled hard hat (from the mill) against the speaker, holding that up with a broom which was supported by a chair which stood on a card table I'd placed on the floor directly beneath the speaker. The whole arrangement tottered uneasily but it held, and the sound was reduced to almost silence. Blessed relief. Everyone cheered *sotto-voce* and tiptoed back to their bunks since any sudden vibration would have been fatal to the stability of our volume control tower. That's when the door opened and Victor came in. He was a little guy, about my size and weight, and he wanted to play cards.

That, I informed him, he could do on his bunk. The card table was being used in an electronic capacity.

He didn't see it that way. He wanted the table.

I said I was sorry, that my heart beat tumultuously for him and that a warm glow of commiseration was suffusing my chest, but that his bunk would have to do for the nonce.

He chose to ignore my point of view and headed for the tower. I unwound myself from my bunk and headed in the same direction, to protect my interests and my sanity. We arrived at the table about the same time.

He laid hands on the broom.

I advised him one last time of the disastrous results any rash act on his part would most certainly produce.

71

The little bugger had spunk, or else he had a tin ear. Even I could hear that I was on the teetering edge of coming totally unglued; I didn't know anything about fighting but anybody knows that a sufficient degree of craziness can take up all kinds of slack in that department. He yanked the broom off the table, the whole contraption collapsed and I almost got hit by the falling hard hat, which bounced twice and rolled underneath the nearest bunk.

I heard the rock music re-explode through the room and felt a similar concussion in my head. I was three feet off the floor and virtually paralled to it when I hit him with a flying tackle that knocked us both onto the bunk under which the hard hat lay. Fists blurred and flew. He seemed as untaught and unpracticed in the arts of war as I; we flailed at each other furiously, recklessly, wholeheartedly; I wanted to murder that guy, I mean just plain *kill* him, simply tear him limb from every possible limb. His inclinations seemed the same. We banged each other's heads on the bunk frames, smashed each other's glasses off, beat each other black and blue. He slid off the bunk onto the floor, I jumped on him and we rolled through the dust and ashes (the huts were heated with old wood stoves) knocking over chairs, boot racks, the card table. It was terrific. It was absolutely marvelous. It was downright ecstatic, is what it was.

That was in fact what finally stopped it. We eventually realized, more or less simultaneously, the extent to which we had actually begun to enjoy the whole debacle. At that point we couldn't take it seriously enough anymore, and quit. He retired to his bunk to repair his glasses while I rebuilt the tower and then proceeded to repair my own. I felt tremendously relieved. Much later he admitted to the same feeling. We'd shaken our first two months in jail a trifle rough.

I was dreaming of women. Oh lord, lots of women, or many of one woman; we were (there seemed many of me as well) all over the beds and on the wharf, talking, laughing, making love so enthusiastically we couldn't even remember our names; that was part of it, a marvelous nameless ecstasy, warm waves glowing around the pilings, a rough shuddering through the timbers, the hand on my shoulder shaking me harshly, insistently, a fist banging on the wall:

"Schroeder! Ass up; wake it 'n shake it!"

Oh Jesus. It has to be too early; the hut is still in a cold gray gloom, I can barely make out the bunks around the room. Gray plywood walls. Has to be too early.

"Getter in gear there, Schroeder; bedding back to the laundry hut, hard hat and gloves in front of the office. Move it!"

Gear and bedding to the . . . Jesus! Instantly wide awake, sun lunging over the horizon, dive off the bunk into the day, everything immediately under way, bedding in a collapsed heap already at the door and a cardboard box, where the hell am I going to find a cardboard box for my stuff? Use Harris's, he won't give a damn, all the papers and old mail, underwear and toilet junk in there and the books, no way I'm doing this in two trips, somehow if I can just get this bedding up with my foot and, why was whoever designed the human body so damned niggardly with hands! Wouldn't have hurt in the least to add a couple more for chrissake.

At the door to the washroom (sign over the door: AB-LUTION HUT. Lord, the stuff that happens when the Corrections Service get their hands on a thesaurus) I dig out my soap and towel and get in there. Two cooks are already shaving by the mirrors. "What the hell you doin up this fuckin early in the goddamn mornin, man?"

I subside onto one of an open bank of toilets and try to keep my downed pants out of the piss on the floor. Still don't feel entirely confortable about taking a crap in public. I always sit there trying to pretend nothing's happening, which is all very well if you have the runs but hardly useful if you have to give the old intestine a little forceful assistance. In a crowd of a dozen guys sitting cheek by jowl on the toilets, you try very hard not to fart so nobody'll notice you're there.

"I said what the fuck you doin up so fuckin early, man?"

I savor the answer as I give it. "Checking out of this dump, man. Leaving home. Going up to Stave."

The cooks are appropriately, cooperatively jealous. "Stave Lake, no shit? Hey hey hey, fat Albert. They work the ass off you up there, man. Eleven hours a day, and no movies."

"Food's the shits, man."

"No pool table, nothin."

I could tell them all about what they can do with their pool table and movies. The main thing is to get out of this hellhole into the bush, as far away as I can get from dormitories and screaming loudspeakers and cantankerous guards and the be-wildering turnover of confused inmates scrabbling through this place every week. If I stay here much longer I'll find myself starting to tell people what I think of them, and I doubt I could handle the echo. Stave Lake Camp, at least, is supposed to be a bit more quiet; a prison logging camp for first offenders with a more stable population and a high ratio of long-timers to short, which always settles a prison down. It's supposed to be harder work up there, I'm told, but less harassment. The guards are older and more experienced, and they stay at the prison forty-eight hours at a stretch to maintain a better level of continuity. They even say there's the odd chance for a weekend temporary absence out of there, although that may be spurious rumor. Who knows? Who ever knows? All you get from the day the gates shut on you is rumor and hearsay; in here you don't believe anyone or anything unless it's on paper, in triplicate and signed by fifteen wardens, the Solicitor General and your fairy godmother. Check for forgeries.

I wipe my ass with paper from the next toilet over and get up gingerly. The cooks have already left.

Outside the Ablution Hut the air is still a frosty gray but the mist is rising in slow, swirling billows off the grass around the flagpole and the spotlight towers.

God but it's beautifully quiet this early in the morning. I feel like I'm drinking in the silence like great draughts of freshly squeezed orange juice. Some bird, sounds like an oriole, is trilling experimentally in the birch over by the office; the only time of day it can make itself heard over the loudspeakers. Go to it, little chirper. Give 'em hell; the whole nine-page opus. Ah yes, that's it, very nice, very nice. Yes, yes, carry on, carry right on . . .

The bullhorn bolted to the office verandah post explodes, I jump about a foot off the ground and drop everything. Wake-up call. Jesus. Almost a month already and I still haven't gotten used to that damned thing. A few seconds later the speakers all around the camp give a brief crackle, then blare

75

into Credence Clearwater Revival's raunchy rendition of "Proud Mary." CKLG is on the case! and another day comes crashing in on Pine Ridge Camp, B.C.

I dig around the scrub by the Ablution Hut door, looking for my toothbrush and razor blades. Had that box so neatly packed, too.

Two of us in a great clattering bread-truck prison van, heading for Stave Lake Camp. Up ahead it looks dreary, ready to rain. The road twists and stutters over old logging-road beds through the mountains; we're having a hard time staying seated on the wooden benches. My stomach's in a turmoil, I'm ecstatic over leaving Pine Ridge, nervous with anticipation over Stave Lake and somewhat nauseous from the jackhammer pounding of the truck's suspension. The other inmate, a heavy-set, quick-witted and unusually articulate Italian named Corso, was in the cell three doors down from me in Oakalla; during the long afternoons when there was nothing to do, I taught him chess and he taught me the deaf-and-dumb sign language. Right now he's cracking his knuckles and snapping his fingers restlessly, more or less in tandem with my stomach and no doubt for similar reasons. I know he's worried about how he'll make out up there. This is the first time he's actually been convicted on a charge, but his arrest record goes back a fair way, and they made it pretty clear to him that his classification to Stave Lake is strictly on a trial basis. As I watch his fingers I suddenly realize with a grin that he isn't snapping them at all, but absent-mindedly shaping the word *shit, shit* . . .

About an hour later the truck heaves into a tight switchback, gears roughly into low and jostles down a steep incline into the camp. What I see is an assortment of aluminum-covered construction trailers crowded into a small forest clearing flanked by soaring evergreens. The whole place seems deserted except for the two uniformed guards who appear out of one of the trailers as the truck rolls to a stop. Corso and I are waved out of the back. The rain has increased to a steady downpour and we're both half soaked by the time we duck into the Administration trailer. We stand on rubber mats in the office, dripping water all over the floor and listening to an introductory lecture. "This camp will be what you make it, etc." Then we follow the guard to a storage room for an issue of raingear.

The raingear, as usual, turns out to be a jumbled assortment of rubber jackets, overalls and boots, all torn and unmatched. Typically, there's only one size available: gargantuan. While we pull the gear over our prison clothes the guard disappears for a minute and returns with two sheets of newspaper and two axes.

"What's this stuff for?"

"Startin forest fires in the rain; what d'you think?"

Back in the truck, the door slams shut and we're off again, this time on a relatively smooth gravel road heading east. The camp turns out to be quite close to the lake; within minutes we arrive at a long, narrow body of water, actually a flooded river rimmed by an unusually wide band of beach. We climb out and pull out the tools, and it's only then that we get a complete view of the place.

"Good Christ!"

"Fan-fucking-tastic!" Corso whistles in astonishment.

78

It looks like the aftermath of a major war. The destruction, in fact, is so massive and so overwhelming it could almost be called magnificent. As far as the eye can see up and down the lake, millions of charred, broken pillars poking up through black water like a bombed, flooded city of ruins. The beach bristles with bleached and water-polished bones. Low black clouds and the driving rain form a heavy somber backdrop, mostly obscuring sullen-looking mountains to the north. Among the beached debris, a scattering of low, guttering fires with stooped black figures moving slowly about them through the smoke, looking like the dying embers and last defeated survivors of some recent holocaust. It reminds me of paintings I've seen of the Plague Days; I can't believe it.

"Take about fifty years to clean all that up." The guard beside me nods, correctly interpreting my amazed look. "And you're gonna do it, kid. Congratulations."

He hands us both the two axes and two pieces of newspaper, pointing to the beach. "In there," he says curtly. "Start a fire. Burn anything that'll burn. Most of it will. Brew-up's in two hours." He climbs back into the truck and drives away, splattering mud in all directions.

I turn to Corso to talk it over. He's still staring at the mess, wide-eyed.

"What d'you think, Corse?"

"Vintage Cecil B. DeMille."

"Yeah."

We lean on our axes for a while, staring at the forbidding scene. Neither of us feels like taking the first step.

"Hey there!"

A figure far down along the beach waves at us, gesticulating with a stick or maybe an axe.

"Fuck 'm," Corse grunts, not moving. "I'm not working in this shit. Nossir, man, not this boy. They can haul me right back to Oakie; at least it's dry in there."

"I think it's a bull, Corse. White hard hat. We better move."

79

"Aw for chrissake!" But he follows anyway, grumbling and cursing at the terrain. We stomp through deep mud, climbing clumsily over great logs and tangled driftwood, sloshing through low pools of slop. Within minutes our boots are full of water and our clothes drenched. My hair keeps plastering across my forehead, and every time I attempt to brush it away I wash more mud into my eyes.

"What the hell you guys think you're here for, a vacation?" The guard who meets us is young, wet and obviously not having the best time of his life either. "Come on, get your asses moving! Quit draggin your tails." He sloshes past and higher up the beach to drier ground, turning back every so often to give us the eye. We begin going through the motions of inspecting logs.

"You got any idea what cedar looks like?"

"I dunno. Sort of reddish, I think."

"Can't tell from the outside; bust one open and look inside."

Corso raises his axe and brings it down on a handy log. The axe sinks into the wood and sticks fast.

"Oh fuck. Now I can't get it out."

"Hold it there. I'll pound it with the back of my axe, like a wedge."

I flip my axe over and hammer on the butt of the buried head. It moves slightly with every blow, but only slightly.

"Hey! Cut that out, you idiot! Stop that! Drop that axe!" The guard comes churning back, waving his arms wildly.

"You don't use an axe like that! Good lord, man, use the peas in your head. You'll crack that steel faster'n you can whistle Dixie! We've got wedges for that; go over and see that guy over there, yeah, that's Larry in the chopped-up hard hat there. He'll give you a couple of 'em."

He flaps his arms against his thighs in an absurd despair. "And try to use your goddamn head from now on. Christ!" He trudges away again, flicking water out of his eyes. I make

80

my way over various stumps and log butts to the inmate with the wedges.

On my way back I see that the guard has stopped to chew out Corso who has sagged behind a stump. I can see him shrugging and pointing helplessly at the buried axe. Finally the guard yells over to another inmate who is operating a chain saw several hundred yards away. By the time I reach the group the guy has bucked up half a dozen lengths of log and freed the axe as well. The guard seems simmered down a bit.

"What's your name? Scroter? Well, now you've got lots of wood bucked up here, enough to keep you busy for at least until brew-up. George here'll lend you his lighter. I wanna see a bonfire that'll roast the balls of god. You two come along with me; we'll find you another place to start. Okay, let's go."

The three of them set off toward the water in search of another batch of cedar; I start to split up the bucked logs they've left behind. Every piece I chop is soaked straight through, a sodden dark brown right to the core. It seems totally pointless, and the paper in my pocket is a sodden mass by this time as well.

I sigh to myself and shrug. What the hell, might as well try. I select a piece of wood and begin to split it down, slicing it into thinnner and thinner sticks, splitting those too until I'm kneeling before a small heap of shredded, slivered splinters. Spindlier than toothpicks. By Jove, that might do it yet.

I carefully build a loose tepee of slightly larger pieces around that. Not bad, not bad at all. Bet old Corse'll never get a fire started in this downpour. I look over to where the three of them are still clustered, the guard pointing energetically toward the ground. Wonder if Corse'll last at all.

I can feel myself falling into that goofy mood I always seem to come up with when things become preposterous or absurd.

I push another handful of splinters under the tepee just in

case. Then I'm ready to go. Hold your breath, all you heavenly hosts in the boundless skies, and you, Lucifer, lay a little brimstone on me, why don't you, old buddy. I shove George's lighter under my architectural marvel and twirl the rasp. Contact! Let her rip!

The shavings hesitate, glimmer demurely for a few seconds and go out. Damn. Have to try that again, shave the shavings even thinner. Threads of cedar is what we need, Monsieur Scrotifer; veritable gossamer threads of cedar. Shouldn't be any problem at all with an axe so blunt, the cutting edge is an eighth of an inch fat. Better use your fingernails. Which is an idea; I'll try that.

An hour and a half later my nails are mostly broken, the lighter is out of fluid and I'm staring down at a sodden little pile of crinkled ashes which represents four different attempts to get wet kindling to burn. I've even tried borrowing some burning driftwood from other fires but the rain puts them out long before I can get back to my shavings again. I'm tired, soaked to the bone, cold and depressed; on top of that, Corso has a roaring fire going a few hundred yards away, keeping warm. Got the chain-saw operator to pour him some oil on his kindling. I'd do it too if I could get away with it, but the guard keeps circling closer and closer to my work site now, obviously increasingly irritated with my failure. I couldn't get my hands on any gas or oil at this stage if I had the money to pay for it.

Finally I stop the useless enterprise for a moment and gaze around, taking stock of the situation. Everywhere I look is exhausted grayness, a depressing listlessness, and here I am, seemingly at its very center, kneeling in black mud up to my ass, shivering in the driving rain and surrounded by great upheavals of tangled wreckage and destruction. The water off my hard hat streams down my neck and visor and onto the remains of the fire that never was.

And it seems to me I've come to some sort of crossroads in

the middle of all this mess. Suddenly, almost effortlessly, I can see that this is what I've been aiming for; this is why I put myself into this place. This is how I've decided to find out what I can really handle, and what I really need to stay alive, what I will finally defend and what suddenly won't be important anymore when the chips are down. This is where I start to find out who I really am.

I gather the useless sticks of cedar and go through the motions again, but it's just a gesture for the guard and to keep my hands occupied; I don't care about the fire anymore. Suddenly it's all very clear, very concise, like many ragged stray thoughts old and new woven together into a hard, clean pattern. All my life I've been speaking in borrowed voices, living on borrowed values, furnishing my head with borrowed ideas, borrowed enthusiasm. I've been loving by proxy and hating by proxy, and I've been skidding across the surface of my life as if it were a sheet of watered glass. And because of that, I've never been driven to any real desperation; I've always been gambling with other people's money.

It has to stop; I've got to come up with some honest answers. I hardly know anything about myself.

Sitting there in the mud and the rain I feel my face stretching into an ironic grin. I guess I've known that for much longer than I've been aware of it; nice of my brain to finally let me in on what it's been doing with my life. Because this certainly is the place to do it in. Out here, I have no history, no character, no name. Out here I'm simply a bedraggled human being in a crowd of other unrecognizable men, all of us scrabbling through a godforsaken landscape trying to hold ourselves up over our own heads so we won't get too wet. Here I'm not obliged to be consistent because there's nothing to be consistent with, and my time is my own because what I do with my hands is not important. As for my thoughts, no one could care less.

Suddenly I'm in a fine mood, an excellent mood. I stem my axe into the mud and push myself to my feet, surveying the beach once more, slowly, from end to end. Who knows? Really, who knows? Maybe in all this mess it'll work. Maybe it'll really happen. Maybe I'll get pushed so hard I'll find myself starting to say things I don't even recognize. Maybe I'll get so bored and so frustrated and so tired and so angry, I'll be left with nothing. Empty. Totally exhausted. I've never been totally exhausted in my life. The idea intrigues. Maybe that's how it'll be. Maybe I'll come out of here simply blank, stripped to the bare walls.

Bemused and preoccupied, I stagger about looking vaguely for a drier piece of cedar, almost bumping into the guard who's come up behind me to see what's going on.

"Still can't get it going, eh?"

His voice has dropped an octave, no doubt in tandem with his estimation of me; the tone is the kind one uses with helpless dolts, resourceless incompetents.

"Don't seem to be having any luck; I've used up all the fluid the lighter had." My voice, I'm not entirely surprised to hear, is almost idiotically cheerful.

"Well, you shoulda stuck your newspaper in your underpants. Best place to keep it dry. Only place, lotta the time." He looks at me closely. "And just what the hell you grinnin about?"

I sweep my hand over the whole scene, luxuriously. "With all this shit, how can a man avoid having a good time?"

He follows my hand with his eyes, over the black ruins, the stumps. Then, unexpectedly, he grins as well. "Well, I've always said it's a great place for a party."

A loud metallic clanging drifts over from the far side of the beach.

"Leave your stuff," the guard says. "You're no damn good at startin fires anyway. Time for brew-up."

Morning here is still the worst part of the day. I've always slept quite soundly and since I've been in prison I've found myself crawling even more deeply into myself in sleep. Unfortunately the wake-up procedure here is much like a frontal tank assault. Our rooms are fitted with brilliant 200-watt bulbs, and at 6:00 A.M. the guards flick them on and pound on the plywood walls shouting our names. So far I've been totally unable to get used to this method; my brain spins and lurches like a many-branched panic and my entire nervous system recoils, crouching and bristling. Often, it doesn't fully relent until noon . . .

It has been raining now for almost four months without pause. The camp lies in a valley surrounded on all sides by high mountains, effectively locking it into a weather pattern that douses it with about two hundred and ten inches of rainfall a year. We live day in and day out in diaphanous raingear, soaked to the skin more often than not and rarely completely warm; even the trailer ceilings leak water, which collects in streams on the floor and has to be mopped regularly with towels and buckets.

Even so, we're apparently living a much better life than our predecessors. According to old historians here, the first inmates who came to this area to build the camp lived for up to six months in tents, often sleeping in wet bedding and wet clothes, and eating outside in the snow or rain.

FRAGMENT

As usual it's pouring rain. We're in the middle of a scrub forest building gravel roads toward the lake. The ditching work done by the back-hoe has proven inadequate; the entire area is a flooded bog and only the roadbed (what there is of it) is solid ground. We've been sent up here to dig drainage ditches through the area by hand; machinery keeps getting buried in the mud.

It's brew-up time. A blackened iron pot hangs over a low fire in the middle of the road. A dozen shovels lie flung into a criss-crossed heap under a nearby tree like so many spat-out curses. The plastic bowls we use to drink the coffee are scattered among the rocks or trampled into the mud. There are seventeen of us today, each man dressed in black raingear, orange hard hat and rubber boots. When the call for brew-up came we threw our shovels onto a pile and rolled pieces of rock or log close to the fire and sat down where we sit now, motionless, collars up and hunched against the rain, which pelts in gusts across the clearing. Nobody says anything. No sound at all except the flurries of wind and the rain spattering on our rubber jackets. Each man lost in thought or blankness, huddled into the recesses or caverns of his mind to wait out the rain before his eyes. Each man under his own rock.

Twenty feet away under a tree the guard crouches beneath a tarp slung between two low-hanging branches; the canvas has holes in it through which the water soaks into his uniform cap. The visor is pulled low over his eyes and water drips off its edge onto his pants. He, too, sits motionless.

- - - -.

The muted growl of a small aircraft intrudes for a few moments over the drumming rain; fades away.

Rain gusts in swirling squalls down over the trees, pockmarking the standing water and prattling against the mud and raingear.

- - - -.

Everywhere gray, mud, cold. In a forest clearing on a ridge of gravel amid uprooted trees and chopped-up logs, seventeen black mounds, unmoving. A tiny damp flame flickers uncertainly in their midst like the last remaining spark of life about to go out. Rain drives in steady wind-blown sheets against the ground. No one says anything.

- - - -.

Sometimes the wind sounds like lengths of wet silk being whisked across strips of raw cedar . . .

At Pine Ridge Camp I worked briefly on the band saw and I liked it. "What the hell you keep lookin so goddamn cheerful for?" a long-timer in charge of chain-saw maintenance growled at me one day. He was clearly furious. "Haven't you got any fuckin manners?"

That's when I began to realize how complicated, even dangerous, it is to express (even feel) joy in jail. You can't simply go throwing it around like hellos and goodbyes. In fact, Inside opinion seems to hold that no inmate has any business feeling good at all, inasmuch as the sight of his joy might make another inmate feel worse than he's already feeling. Therefore it's important to feel whatever little joy you might find Inside very cautiously, to say the least.

Whistling, as I've said, is definitely out; inmates become extremely hostile toward whistlers. Singing falls into the same category, generally speaking, although occasionally a guitar will be permitted into prison and then the playing or singing of blues might be tolerated, as long as it's not done too exuberantly. Some prisons have special soundproof rooms for the playing of instruments.

What it really all boils down to is something like courtesy; you don't take an inmate who's shaking it rough and rub his nose in the spectacle of your good humor. To cover all possibilities, therefore, the most all-purpose expression to wear Inside is a loose half-frown, a vaguely dissatisfied grimace, which reassures those doing hard time that they're not the only ones having troubles. It also takes up the slack when you begin genuinely to feel that way yourself.

As for the joy connected with an inmate's imminent release, this understandably requires much effort on both sides and is therefore the most difficult to handle. The inmate about to leave is of course obliged to mask or at least suppress his happiness as much as possible, to speak only in careless and maybe even bored tones about his upcoming plans and to refrain from speaking of them at all in the presence of long-timers. Those remaining behind, on the other hand, must learn to withstand the onslaught of his bright face and eyes as calmly as they can; one of the first and very important defenses against depression which an inmate must learn Inside is to placidly countenance a fellow inmate's departure.

There is, as a matter of fact, a tradition that comes to the aid of both sides in this situation: as soon as an inmate's release has been announced or confirmed (usually several weeks in advance), all other prisoners slowly begin to fall away from him, his allies scout around for new supporters, he is no longer automatically included in bull sessions or meetings to plan inmate events (both legal and illegal), and he is no longer obliged (or encouraged) to become involved in "political" matters, arguments between other inmates or any of the usual assortment of pranks or projects under way at any time inside a prison. Eventually, only those whose time is also nearing its end still sit with him at meals or after work. There is no particular disloyalty in this, and certainly no ill will; it is simply a standing, almost unconscious policy developed over generations and found to be safest for all concerned. Safest not only with reference to the emotional stability of those remaining behind, but also because the end of a man's sentence often makes him careless, and information carried to the Outside has the annoying habit of sometimes causing unexpected trouble for those left Inside.

None of which is meant to imply that you don't go out of your way to find a bit of joy in prison—you do, and when you find it, you mine it mercilessly, squeezing every last drop you can possibly squeeze from it. But you must do it secretly, secretly . . .

FRAGMENT

29

Pok. Chick. Pling. Chlok. Axe heads rise and fall in irregular rhythm over bucked log ends in a clearing just off the main lake road. We're scattered along a dried-up creek bed just above the bridge, chopping firewood for the Forest Service.

A light rain has been drizzling steadily all morning, hazing the clearing with a gray gauze that reduces visibility by blurring rather than blocking. Fifty yards away I can barely see the dim shape of the guard sitting on a stump smoking a cigarette. I'm soaked through to my underwear and totally numbed, chopping mechanically, my thoughts off elsewhere, drifting; chanting, I suddenly realize, the McDonald Hamburger ditty:

> *"Who's the McFunniest man in the land?*
> *Who's the McWhackiest—give him a hand! ..."*

which just keeps reeling like some babbling drunk through my mind. I try to trip it up somehow, think determinedly of things useful, things pending, but the second I drop my attention it surges back:

*Whose feet are funniest, whose drinks are yummiest?
Ronald! Ronald McDonald!"*

The commercial is finally buried by the sounds of a heated argument several yards away, where two inmates are threatening each other with raised axes over a question of (as far as I can tell) who is the more manly:

"Yeah? Well, I don't screw dogs an' goats like you do, turtle-fucker!"

"Aw kiss my fruit-loop, jackass!"

"Here! All right now, break it up! Get your goddamn fruity-toots or turtle-butts or whatever back to work! I see one more raised axe around here today and you can both dry off in the Hole!"

The guard grinds his cigarette stub into the mud and spits purposefully before reassembling himself on his stump. The rain drizzles on.

(This morning at breakfast they hounded a young newcomer mercilessly from table to table in search of a place to sit. Nobody had told him that each inmate has a permanent seat and he began by simply sitting down on the nearest vacant bench. The arrival of its owner flushed him out of it like a frightened grouse, but the one on which he settled next only earned him the same response, and he was out in the aisle again, clumsily balancing his plate, cup and cutlery, helplessly looking for his cue. There was none; the guards were still outside and he hadn't yet secured any allies. There was finally nothing for it but to sit on the floor in the aisle and endure the cursing and extravagant stumblings of the incoming inmates as they arranged to fall over him on their way to their seats, spilling syrup over his hair and sausages down his neck. Then someone planted a hobnailed boot directly on his plate, squishing pancakes, eggs and broken glass in a wide smear across his lap. The kid reared up off the ground with an odd, half-choked sort of gasp, his breakfast and the

93

broken crockery cascading to the floor as he bolted for the door. He almost didn't make it through; the cook leaped to cut him off but stumbled on a floor mop and missed.)

The inmate tending brew fire suddenly bangs a broken axe on the pot and calls for coffee. Axes are abandoned in mid-swing, saws choked in mid-cut; the air is suddenly filled with the flurried loose-change jingle of ill-fitting rubber boots scrambling through the drifts of creek-bed pebbles to the road. In the scuffle to get first coffee someone kicks the stack of plastic bowls across the mud; clouds of curses billow over the heads and shoulders as the dishes are retrieved and wiped with torn shirt sleeves and shirt tails. I stand back and wait for the mayhem to subside; to stick one's bowl into that flurry of dunking crockery would be to ask for a splash of scalding coffee over one's hand.

And standing back happen to notice Nevil, a thirty-five-year-old Torontonian ex-salesman with a penchant for stringing mandalas and reading Russian novels, staring at the scene before him in half-cynical disbelief, a head-shaking look in his eyes as he scans from left to right and our eyes meet. Just for a second, little more than an instant of recognition, and then both of us just crack up, just let go and convulse with laughter; a rueful, helpless, slightly woeful and exasperated hilarity that seems to want to go on and on. And my mind fingers over the beads once more, the "What am I *doing* here?" "What *is* this?" "I can't believe I'm *seeing* all this shit" and "Where the hell *am* I?"

From his self-mocking expression I can see that Nevil, too, has seen it all again today, and is chanting the same liturgy . . .

FRAGMENT

30

Once we got to Stave Lake, something odd began to happen to Corso. He began to change as if some new chemical had been poured into him; he became loud, pushy, offensive; he seemed to have made an instant hit with the camp toughs and the older inmates in the place. When those of us who knew him at Oakalla happened to be sitting together during one of his increasingly frequent show-off performances, we just looked at each other and frowned, puzzled. He certainly had had us all thoroughly fooled.

When I first met Corso in Oakalla he was bunked in drum nineteen, three cells down from mine. He was of medium height, overweight and worried. He said he'd left his Street affairs in bad shape and was facing trouble; his girl had run off with his bank account and he owed some heavy money to some heavy people. It all involved paper-hanging—fake credit cards, rubber checks—and a bit of enforcement: he'd been a collector for some family or other.

It was the paper-hanging he'd finally been arrested for, quite suddenly and before he'd been able to deliver the week's collections which he'd stashed in a safety-deposit box. Only his girl friend had a key. When she suddenly stopped visiting him and a family member showed up instead, Corso started to sweat. The family made kindly enquiries about money they should already have had in their possession. Corso began to brood on his bunk restlessly, snapping his fingers and smacking his fists into his palms, the perfect picture of a man in a bad jam. He didn't ask for help and didn't seem to want any, for which reason all kinds of people offered it to him. He refused most of it outright and nibbled only briefly at the rest.

One day he showed us a scar on his belly from a bullet wound, describing a scene in which, during a heated argument with his girl, he'd thrown a revolver on the table and shouted at her to kill him if she hated him so much. His face pulled into an exasperated grin and his eyes flashed a mixture of outrage and delight. "You know," he said, still astonished half a year after the event, "the little cunt actually grabbed the piece and shot me. Blew a slug right into my gut. Fuck!" We all sat around nodding; that was impressive. She sounded like a spunky chick. "And now," Corso scrunched his mouth to one side, disappointed, slightly woeful, "the dumb bitch fucks off with a stack of hot money that's goin to get her legs broke and her face busted in. Christ!"

We all nodded again; that was a poor performance. She sounded like she hadn't gotten it straight that time. But what was left unsaid because it didn't need to be said was that Corso's legs were also involved; the money had been his responsibility. Corso sat back on his bunk again, continuing his worried twitch. Somebody clapped him on the back and offered him a game of chess.

I honestly can't remember precisely how it was that we became friends. Something about him interested me; he was astonishingly articulate when he wanted to be, and nimble-minded; he spoke four languages (English, French, Italian

96

and Cree) and knew the dactylology of deaf-mutes as well; he'd traveled widely and described his travels imaginatively and often surprisingly concisely. He often came over to ask for this or that piece of advice. He said he wanted to learn to write. "I'm tired of having people listen to me only because I can beat the shit out of them," he told me, flexing his fingers in an ambiguously practiced manner. "I want people to listen to me because I express myself well." It sounded like a good idea at the time.

We began reciprocal lessons. I taught him English composition and he taught me the deaf-mute sign language; in between we often played chess, discussed women, literature, crime and metaphysics. Coincidentally, both of us had recently broken up with long-time mistresses and we spent a lot of time comparing notes, marveling at the mysterious compulsions and delusions that confuse the relationships between men and women. He described his fever-chart life on the Street, the back-alley beatings, the con games, the credit swindles, the gambling rackets; the endless surges and collisions of fast-buck hustlers constantly on the move, matching wits and muscles, hoarding and spending like frantic children on a circus spree. I described my driftings through the Lebanese and Syrian deserts with the Bedouins, the outlaw villages of the mountains and the smugglers' routes that crisscross the Middle East like the hidden wires of a vast and secret telephone system. We compared families and futures and values and ideals; we haggled over methods and purposes and what was the point. We played a lot of basketball.

I'm still not entirely sure what it was that stopped me from trying to raise the money to get him out of his jam. Certainly that was the intention of the game, and certainly the impulse was there many times, like the guilty stirring of one's conscience, that automatic compulsion to help a fellow man in obvious need which, if not followed, makes one feel like a heel when the opportunity is past. As in the most clever setups, all the urgency about the money seemed to come from me; I was the one busily trying to figure out how I could raise enough to make any difference, to buy him at least enough time to be able to use his own ingenuity to raise the rest.

It was superbly professional, and principally so because Corso not only used shrewd observation and crafty technique, but also threw *himself* into the bargain. He used his own weaknesses and strengths, his own fascinations and boredoms, all of which were entirely real and subverted only to the extent that they would always be abruptly interrupted or ended whenever the jig was up. It may be that such men have a second set of everything, of sensibilities, of feelings, even of values, but if so, they certainly don't seem to get much time to use it. The dimensions of their con game seem in most cases (as I was later to observe in more detail) to be virtually equal to that of their everyday lives.

Whatever the reason, some faint but persistent doubt restrained me each time I teetered on the edge of committing myself and my resources, a fact that puzzled and even irked me to such an extent that I at one point considered facing him outright on the subject, asking him to comment on the curious uncertainty his manner evoked in me. Finally, however, I did nothing and simply kept my peace, riding out the undertow uncomfortably but doggedly, very unhappy over my own seemingly ungracious misgivings. Much later a chance remark to a mutual acquaintance gave the whole show away (". . . three months on that bastard, and all I got was talk . . ."), but by then I'd already come to the same conclusion on my own.

That, however, was later; in the meantime there were still the Classification hurdles to clear, the interviews to determine the security level at which each inmate was to do his time. When the calls began to come through I was one of the first on the list, and when I'd been trotted through the obscure and somewhat hurried process, I was informed that I'd been consigned to a certain Stave Lake Camp. Nobody knew anything specific about the place except that it was generally considered to be pretty stable and a reasonable place to do long time. Later that afternoon Corso sagged into the tier and announced unhappily that he'd been rejected on his Stave Lake application; his previous arrest record made him ineligible for the place. Stave Lake Camp, it turned out, was a first-offenders' prison logging camp, and Corso wasn't exactly a first offender.

This was, however, his first conviction, so we filed an appeal, stressing that point as well as the fact that he'd been working with me in English composition and that he intended to continue these lessons if the Stave Lake application was approved. Surprisingly, the Classification Board accepted the appeal on the basis of my university background, and when we were eventually herded into two trucks for the transport down the valley to H.C.C. and Stave Lake, Corso was on board. Unfortunately, we all ended up bogged down first in Haney, then Pine Ridge Camp, waiting for accommodation to become available at Stave. Some of us never did make it to that camp.

It was at Pine Ridge Camp that Corso did me a last big favor. After nineteen days in that place, word leaked out that two slots were opening up at Stave. That evening, just before supper, Corso slipped into Hut Six and whispered to me that he and Walter Banson had been chosen to go. Banson was a young executive who had juggled the funds; he had come to Pine Ridge two weeks previously on the same classification. Strictly speaking, I (and the rest of our bunch) had five days' seniority on the man, although the Administration seemed to be dealing with their waiting list alphabetically. I pointed this out to Corso.

He agreed, assured me he'd take care of the matter, and did. Next morning he and I were rousted out of our beds at twilight, urged through a hasty breakfast and locked into a bread-truck van headed for Stave Lake. Two weeks later we were for all intents and purposes enemies.

It happened so strangely, so smoothly, that I'm still not sure I understand all that went on in the man's head. Soon after we'd both put in several days on the beach, Corso was suddenly shifted to the Shake Crew, a group of senior inmates who scouted the surrounding forest for old cedar logs, which they cut into three-foot lengths and split into blocks for cedar shakes. It was preferred work, minimally supervised although hard, and Corso was chosen mainly because of his heavy build; the Shake Crew badly needed a sledge-hammer driver.

The shift, however, was also an unprecedented "promotion" for a new arrival, a sudden and exhilarating boost up the hierarchical ladder which rather went to Corso's head. Within days, in abrupt, almost larval stages, he molted, enlarged and metamorphosed from a dangerous but passive (and worried) defender into a dangerous, active and very confident aggressor, brash and swaggering and constantly acting the buffoon. From my particular vantage point it seemed that Corso was careening dangerously close to the edge of whatever he was capable of handling, but then I hadn't even suspected the side of him that was now in full view, so I said nothing. For all I knew there were even more sides to him than these.

Naturally, his quick ascent polarized much of the Stave Lake inmate population. Many who had been overtaken muttered angrily, while those on top of the pile inspected this new upstart casually but carefully, decided he was made of recognizable stuff and permitted him to stay. He got along well with them and played them cautiously, being careful to restrict his bluster only to those whom he had already outdistanced. As the Beach and Shake crews tended to avoid each other both on and off the job, Corso and I also saw less and less of each other as the days passed. I was myself increasingly busy with the writing workshop I was setting up in camp, and he became involved in a lot of card tournaments, which his group was staging regularly in the mess hall during the evenings. It got so that we saw each other only occasionally during meals, when chance threw us together on the food queue; on such occasions we made perfunctory conversation, but there was a peculiar deadness between us that I couldn't explain.

Then, several weeks later, things took a drastic turn, although it wasn't immediately obvious at the time. One day at the beach while we were burning driftwood in the usual pouring rain, the deputy warden's truck pulled up above our work site and the warden waved to a guard. The guard joined him in brief conference, then called for me. At the truck the warden asked me if I'd studied English. I said I had.

"Can you write reports, progress reports, production reports and forecasts, that sort of thing?"

"I suppose so."

"Okay, get inside."

He drove me back to camp and set me up in an unused storage room with typewriter, desk and stacks of production statistics to interpret. "Write a story," he said, pointing to the figures. "Make it sound good." Then he drove off.

I sat staring at the typewriter. The job was hardly an unmixed blessing. True, I was in out of the rain, but to work so directly for the Administration was a potentially dangerous business and I wasn't overly interested in getting involved in any hassles. The safest jobs in prison are always those which keep you both far from the guards and close to the other inmates; in such work one is least susceptible to accusations of "collaborating." If there's one Inside neurosis that takes precedence over all others, it's the constant suspicion of being surrounded by "rats," a suspicion that is not only paranoid, it's often true. I opened the door a crack, checked the corridor and hurried over to the Tool Room. Richard Belaire, a senior inmate and chain-saw mechanic, presided over his kingdom there.

"Hey, Richard."

He looked up from a chain-saw he was breaking down and flashed me an ambiguous grin. "Yeah, I heard about your new job," he said wryly. "Movin closer to the fire where it's warm?"

"Fuck that. I didn't ask for this job. But I'd sure appreciate it if you'd proof it for me."

Belaire pursed his lips. "This thing gonna be steady?"

"He didn't say."

Belaire got up and checked the corridor with a practiced glance. He was as interested as anyone else in "additional information" of any kind. "All right," he said. "Let's go."

In the storage room I showed him everything the Warden had left behind. Belaire checked it all carefully, puzzling over the figures and snickering where he knew them to be padded. Every several minutes he threw a glance along the corridor.

"Yeah, this shit's okay. Nothin here except lies about how many squares of shake blocks and split shakes we produced last year. I can vouch for this all right."

"Good; thanks. Needless to say, drop in any time and browse around."

Belaire disappeared back down the corridor and I started to work, satisfied that I'd covered myself in the appropriate manner.

But I'd relaxed too soon. Three days later the rumor was afloat that I'd had "access to inmate files," and the camp population began to polarize along some very strange lines. Initially, I didn't know enough about what I'd run into until an older inmate took me aside and clarified the obvious.

"Some of these guys aren't exactly in here for the reasons they claim," he explained, faintly annoyed at my newness. "You told me yourself about that skinner in the truck. Well, some of these guys are in here for the same beef but they're

102

telling everybody "manslaughter" or "violence with intent" or some such thing. For pretty obvious reasons, eh? So now there's this rumor that you've seen the files and they're scared for their asses. They've gotta discredit you in case it's true. Incidentally, what's this guy Corso got against you, anyway?"

"Corso? Is Corso in on this?"

The older man looked at me quizzically, then gave me a dry grin. "What d'you mean, 'in on it'? He's the bloody source of it, for fuck's sake!"

The next two weeks were bad. Tension kept building as more and more inmates joined the dispute and gravitated to one side or the other. I tried on several occasions to face Corso directly with the issue, inviting him to openly accuse me and lay down his "facts" or stop all this malicious rumor-spreading. Most prisons, in fact, recognize the danger that uncontrolled hearsay represents by establishing a special committee of senior inmates whose specific job it is to track down such gossip and determine its validity; they call them the "rumor-squelchers." But Stave Lake Camp had no such committee and of course Corso wasn't the least bit interested in clarifying anything. A "cause" like this was just what he needed to round out his drive to establish undisputed seniority, and he played it to the hilt. He began working his way through the camp like a politician, shaking hands and back-slapping, scattering benign crumbs of pleasantries among the newcomers who were inclined to be astonished and delighted at this unexpected attention from the higher ranks. He warned them in comradely fashion to keep clear of certain people who just might be working for the Administration and who couldn't therefore be trusted, who were probably at this very moment poring over their records and scheming to blackmail them all, etc.

At first I just stood back and sneered; I refused to believe that anybody would be conned for long by such obvious tactics. A week or so later, however, I wasn't at all so sure, and soon after that, after a newcomer felt confident enough to physically threaten me in a clothes-change line-up, I knew I was wrong. It was becoming clear that I was being boxed into a corner, my inaction being interpreted as a tacit admission of defeat, which somehow amounted to an admission of guilt. I realized that if I didn't do something soon, I'd probably end up with a broken head or back in the cells, or both.

The problem of being the victim of an unjust attack in prison, however, is a tricky one, particularly if you're not in a position to resolve it promptly by simply knocking your opponent's block off. For one thing, the dispute must remain secret, since calling on the authorities is absolutely out of the question. Secondly, as with most prisons, Stave Lake Camp subscribed to a curious (and quite informal) system of Inside justice amounting essentially to a policy of "winner take all." There is, despite its obvious philosophic shortcomings, a practical reason for this: in a survival of the fittest situation, losers invariably cause problems for everyone, being as they are virtually sitting ducks for the provocations of hoodlums who smell out a victim as instantly as a predator scents its prey.

"Whatever else is true," a guard once explained to me, "losers become statistics, bad statistics, and that screws up our records and our morale." Invariably, when guards broke up a fight or mopped up after one had taken place, the winner was briefly punished but the loser was transferred to the cells and never came back. Being "transferred to the cells" in this case meant losing one's minimum-security rating and being returned to maximum security at Haney. And that was a hell of a place to do one's time.

(There was, incidentally, one way to break that rule from an underdog position: if you were a cook, a mechanic or an operator of machinery vital to the prison's maintenance or labor program, you were informally but for all intents and purposes "under protection." One of the not altogether facetious maxims I used to hear Inside was that if you'd been arrested for a crime and were facing near-certain imprisonment, delay your trial long enough to finish a cooking course; cooks in prison virtually wrote their own tickets and were given instant "seniority.")

I was, in short, slipping into a precarious position; that was becoming obvious. I had to protect and consolidate my position more effectively, to secure more allies and, ideally, to make myself somehow indispensable. The solution occurred to me by accident one evening, when an inmate came to the writing workshop to ask for help with his parole application. Like most inmates, he was functionally illiterate and incapable of clearly formulating his future plans in the proper Parole-Boardese. I happened to have developed a knack for that particular jargon, as well as the argot of the Review Boards, which considered applications for temporary leaves and day paroles. Plus: I had access to a typewriter. I'd watched cell mates scrawling illegible sentences across application forms and suddenly I knew the value of such a machine. My route was now abundantly clear.

I spread the word that I might be willing to compose articulate paragraphs for all inmates who were filling out applications for anything at all, and to type them out properly on my old Underwood.

Just as I'd suspected, the effect of the offer was virtually instant. Almost overnight I was filling out four or five applications an evening, sending out a steady stream of clean, legible forms which must have surprised the Parole and Review Boards a good deal, and which certainly seemed to impress them since we soon noted a definite increase in the number of applications granted.

All of which went some distance to right my formerly lopsided situation, but the upshot was that Corso angrily redoubled his efforts and I promptly redoubled mine, both of us now grimly entrenched in our peculiar little war, which was splitting the camp in two. By a curious coincidence, most of the participants in the writing workshop were bunked in the same barracks as I, and most of the members of Corso's work gang were bunked in his, with the result that the two sets of barracks at Stave also became the two opposing territories of the feud. Visiting between Huts One and Two (as they were called) dwindled considerably, and those actively involved in the controversy tended to enter opposing huts in two's and three's, or only very briefly and inconspicuously.

At noon when work stopped and we gathered around our fires for lunch, the issue became the main topic of conversation, although I soon noted that nobody seemed overly concerned about the actual *reason* for the issue—everyone seemed far more interested in the opportunity to establish a particular identity, to belong to a particular group. In fact, I had eventually to realize that their falling in with me had less to do with me or my difficulties than with the handy opportunity to get involved in a cause, any cause—a cause being demonstrably more interesting than no cause at all, and giving anyone who needed it an excuse to take a few pot shots at someone else who might have been bugging him for some reason. On the other hand, I could at least rest assured that I had people I could call on in case of trouble, and I could work without wearing a metal plate on my back or having to maintain a constant lookout for accidentally flying axes or falling trees—I was still working outside part of the time at this stage.

Then, several days later, an inmate from down the hall rushed into my room and told me that Corso and his bunch were meeting in the dining room and he didn't like the sound of things. They sounded as if they were tired of sitting around and wanted to *do* something, and did I think we should call some people together. I decided to wait and watch, suggested he sneak back to the dining room to eavesdrop on the rest of the meeting there, and drifted over to another inmate's room where a number of our hut's people were playing chess. I mentioned the meeting in the dining hall and then got involved in a game myself, all of us keeping a casual but constant watch on the door. An hour later the inmate from the dining room returned and reported that the meeting was over.

"So what went down over there? What're they up to?"

"I think they went a bit spinny or something—they put a contract out on you, man. Fifteen choney bars, to beat up, not to kill."

"Well, I'll be fucked."

My first impulse was to snicker. Fifteen chocolate bars sounded altogether too silly; it made the whole undertaking sound like a child's game, like some goofy joke. More experienced inmates felt otherwise; they pointed out that fifteen bars represented over a week's wages and were the standard currency Inside. That was how Inside "jobs" of any kind were paid for: in canteen goods or returned favors. Besides, it was only a contract to change someone's facial geography, not to take someone's life.

"Still, who'd be stupid enough to risk it?" I wanted to know, looking around at the inmates in the room. "Who'd actually risk another half-year in the slammer for a lousy week's pay?"

I got my answer just after supper two days later, and I realized it the instant G.E. (he was nicknamed General Electric; "short-circuited like a burned-out dildo" one inmate had pointed out) stepped into my room.

"Jesus Christ, G.E.!" I flung at him, about-facing and backing against the wall while looking for something to throw. "You're doing your last six days; you're even goofier than your reputation if you sell that away for fifteen chonies. Use your goddamn head, man!"

G.E. was huge, powerful and mentally only half his own

107

age; I doubted that he was even listening. He stepped the remaining several feet into the room and reached for my shirt front; I dodged and jumped backward onto the bed. "You called me a goof," he glowered sullenly, as if psyching himself into a righteous rage. "You called me a goof behind my back. People been telling me." He made another grab, which I barely managed to evade. "You know what I'm gonna hafta do to you? You know what I do to guys what call me a goof?"

"You going to line up the whole damn camp and make something of it?" I demanded, trying to stall for time and wondering how they'd ever managed to put him up to it. "*Everybody* in this camp calls you a goof, G.E.; they've been calling you that since the day you got here—to your face, your back, your head and your ass. Why suddenly so sensitive?"

I didn't get time to find out; G.E. hurled himself without further warning across the bed and tore me onto the floor, my kicks to his arms and midriff apparently without effect. And then he just as suddenly reared away with a howl, and from my nether view I saw a gallery of faces: Frenchie, Chuck, Bernie and even old Joe the Cleaner, all red-faced and bright with the excitement of battle, and Frenchie had G.E. in some exotic form of hammerlock and was doing rather intolerable things (judging by G.E.'s desperate bellowing) to his right ear, Bernie was jumping up and down furiously shouting, "Get outta my way, get outta my way, for chrissake; lemme give 'm a few!" while Chuck was busily delivering a string of swift kicks to G.E.'s legs and rear. I staggered to my feet through a shower of books, which were toppling off a dislodged bookshelf, and after repeated attempts finally managed to slow the brawl long enough to let G.E. escape. To have beaten him to any visible extent would have been asking for the same trouble he had risked in coming to do the same to me.

G.E. disappeared hastily, and we all sat back on stools and

108

my bunk, delightedly re-enacting and redescribing the scene again and again. We knew the news was spreading through the camp and expected the guards to show any time, but we didn't care—for the moment at least, it felt as if it had all been worth it. And to everyone's surprise the guards never did show up, although I couldn't believe they hadn't caught at least some wind of the whole affair. Possibly they simply decided to let things ride, inasmuch as G.E. was leaving in a short while anyway and there was little point of smudging camp records.

In any case, the story even has a surprise ending in that, as a result of the contract business, a number of senior inmates decided to investigate Corso's allegations themselves and subsequently pronounced them unfounded, which collapsed Corso's cause completely. To my utter astonishment he apologized for the whole affair, and although we never again got past the stage of reticent politeness, that was the end of the feud I'd never really fully understood.

As it turned out, in fact, I gained quite considerably by the whole mess, since it left me in an extremely secure position, which was never again seriously threatened by anyone and which even safely survived a stint in solitary confinement, described in Fragment 39.

FRAGMENT

31

There were five of us that particular evening. We'd been cleared by one of the guards on duty to jog down to the lake shore and were resting on various stumps and logs when Mieszko pulled out a joint. "Party time," he said with a smirk. "Got it through the oil delivery dude." That briefly put everyone into a quandary.

As you might imagine, the bulls didn't let simply anyone out of camp; the ones let out were generally the ones who tended to come back. They were also the ones whose records were relatively clean and who intended, more or less, to keep them that way. On the other hand, the prospect of a little smoke was undeniably mind-watering, and the risks seemed slight. We talked it over and decided we'd smoke the joint, but that on arrival back at camp Chuck would report to the guard for us all, while the rest would go straight to bed. And no goddamn giggling either, by Jesus!

We bunched into a tight group and Greg lit the joint, passing it around. For the next five minutes nobody spoke; sounds only of deep inhaling and exhaling, low grunts and

110

the odd ahhh . . . hhh . . . Then it was down to a shred, the last man burned his fingers as a frugal man should and Chuck buried the left-over paper. We sat around on the stumps idly, nobody particularly talking. One thing about the B.C. bush: it's so damned picture-postcard everywhere you look, but it knocks you out anyway, no matter how many times you've seen it. There it really is, I remember thinking, feeling extremely pleased with my eyes, ears and nose.

"Anybody lit yet?" That was Chuck, always the statistician. Basically wanted to run his life like a perpetual labor union meeting. Take a count of absolutely everything. I don't recall whether anybody answered him or not. Possibly someone suggested we'd better be getting back to camp; at least after a time I realized we were all jogging back up the road, drifting slowly through the mottled shadows. Everything was very still.

Then everything was very still again, and I remember thinking (no, having thought) at some point that I'd been thinking about trumpets. A very long time about trumpets. Miles Davis: *Bitches Brew*. That's why I was grinning from ear to ear; I hadn't heard that piece in a long time. I turned to tell Dan about it and he wasn't there; in fact, we were scattered all over the road as far back as a quarter of a mile.

Strange. I kept feeling as if there were something fairly important to keep in mind, yet the infinitely graceful way the trees curved over the road like the soaring arches of some emerald cathedral insisted on all my attention. Astonishing, really. Jesus, it was bloody marvelous. These enormous plants, swaying way up there in an easy wind, their tips deeply submerged in sky . . . bugs, birds, airplanes buzzing about their leaves . . . and the light, the light, the misty spray of quietly shattering glass . . .

A long time just watching the shards of it glistening through the air . . .

And then, without warning, the realization that we were

111

probably in trouble. We were too far stoned; the grass must have been soaked in something. I hadn't even given it a thought when Mieszko pulled out the joint. Now we seemed miles apart, each man already well adrift inside himself, mechanically setting foot before foot, the movements languid, almost underwater, each man totally oblivious to the rest, already beyond calling . . .

I stopped just short of the last corner and headed off each man as he came.

It was like a shock of recognition: we were no longer the same group. Since we had left the lake an immeasurable amount of time had passed; so much time that we had already reached the stage of having forgotten or abandoned the conventions, the tacit agreements, the protocols that had kept us a functioning unit. There was no avoiding it; we were all strangers again, even more so than we had been the first time we'd met in the cell blocks. And though I don't believe we were particularly unwilling to regroup, the immensity of the effort needed seemed to have become apparent to all, and it was a hopelessly daunting prospect. Inside myself I could hear myself cursing, and the echo. I had known this, I had known this; of the strangleweed just beneath the surface of our laughter and comradeship; the moment when it is no longer enough, when it is no longer possible to uphold.

As I looked about me at all those strange creatures floating around my body in worried confusion, I felt suddenly overwhelmed by such an acute sense of aloneness, my entire body ached through every muscle and nerve. Suddenly, again, nothing at all was given; whatever connection had existed between me and them, between me and any human being, unraveled and separated so inexorably, I felt at a stroke homeless, within moments nameless, in a short time finally a thing without shape or grace. All I could see around me was unbridgeable darkness, myself in the middle of my blackest black, all of us the centers of our own blindnesses, weakly

112

trying to radiate our anger, our love, our fear. Jesus Christ, we needed miracles, miracles! Our sense of rightfully belonging in the world was straining at a hawser with all its strands severed but one; everything around us soared and threatened, everyone's instincts were obsolete, our responses uncomputable; that was the message and some of us already knew it was true.

It was frightening. We stood under those huge, menacing flowers and stared helplessly into one another's faces, passing it around (and around). The bulging fat, the thinly elongated terror. We were seeing the enemy and he was truly us, but he was unreachable; at our feet the pool that reflected us all was missing his face, and for each man the missing face was his own. We couldn't move until it appeared.

We waited an interminable time. Waited interminably, hoping one of us would see whatever he had to see to snap us out of this mesmerized state and get us moving again. And finally somebody did, or else it finally didn't matter anymore, and we were suddenly walking around the last corner of the road toward the prison, each man already busily arranging himself to fit the shape he felt he'd left behind in the guard's memory.

I think the ease with which we did that was the final blow. When I made mention of the incident well over a month later (three of us sitting in Mieszko's room patching raingear) there was only an uncomfortable silence, and then Mieszko said somewhat lamely, "Well, like, I'll be fucked if I know what was really happenin out there, man," and soon after that Chuck started talking about cars.

FRAGMENT

32

"One thing I really can't tolerate though," he said almost apologetically, leaning back against the wall and staring at the ceiling with a puzzled frown, "is spiders. I can't find any explanation for it. Something about them drives me totally psycho. If someone were ever to drop a spider down my back, I'm sure I'd completely lose my mind." And something about the quiet way he said that made you believe exactly what he was saying, because Richard Faber didn't throw words around loosely. He listened carefully and spoke the same way, and he wasn't given to exaggeration.

The conspicuous thing about Faber was that he was a gentleman. He was courteous. He was polite. He said please and thank you and he stood aside for you at the door. He was fair in his dealings with everyone, high or low, and he tended to give everyone the benefit of the doubt. He was always neatly dressed and his quarters impeccably ordered; he was cheerful and helpful and dependable in a crunch. Faber was a bank robber who was just finishing an eighteen-month sentence for a credit-union job in Edmonton, plus a little breaking and entering on the side.

From the first day I met him, Faber puzzled me thoroughly. He simply didn't *look* like any sort of criminal I'd ever met. Nor, for that matter, did he act or talk like one. He wasn't even a con man, using his disarming appearance to wheel and deal in that usefully gray area which separates strictly legal from illegal acts. He was simply a handsome and very likeable thirty-five-year-old ex-farmer from Saskatchewan with a modest penchant for knocking over banks and trafficking in stolen property. He never boasted about his exploits, hardly ever talked about them in fact, and maintained a quiet and respected place among the camp elite for no particular reason anyone could name. Yet it wouldn't have occurred to anyone to challenge him.

I talked to him on several occasions, trying to find out just what could have motivated this man to jump into a life of crime. He had no excessive enthusiasms or desires that one could readily see; he didn't seem driven by any unusual compulsions. He was, in fact, remarkably *even*, and not in a forced or faked way either; he seemed genuinely relaxed and cheerful as a rule. He didn't try to evade my questions but insisted he really didn't know the answers; he and his two brothers had simply decided to leave the farm one day and have a bit of a look at the rest of the world. Three months later they'd spent all their money and needed more, and the bank seemed the logical place to get it. There was no history of lawlessness in the family, and aside from the odd Saturday night drunk-tank episode, none of the three had had any run-ins with the law before.

Nevertheless, they somehow acquired several sticks of dynamite and blew away the rear wall of the bank's vault, plunging in through the smoke and rubble to load up sixty-five thousand dollars in cash. Incredibly, they got away with it. By the time the police got to the scene the three were already well out of town, contentedly divvying up the loot. It seemed like a handy way to pay the bills. Several weeks later they did it again, in a different town, and then for the hell of it they broke into a few houses. That didn't pay as well as banks, of course, but it was a darn sight less risky.

With any other inmate it wouldn't even have occurred to me to ask, but Faber seemed a different sort. Didn't he feel it was wrong, this robbing and boosting of people's private possessions? Did he propose to justify it as an act of guerrilla warfare, an attack on the capitalistic system, a "redistribution of wealth" or any of the other convenient ideologies so regularly espoused by an increasing number of petty rip-off artists? Faber looked at me kindly but with just a faint hint of derision. "Of course not," he said quietly. "I wouldn't propose anything of the sort."

"Then what's the rationale?"

Faber gave me an almost benign look this time. "There is no rationale," he said. "It's just plain wrong."

His voice wasn't the least bit defensive, but also clearly implied no interest whatsoever in haggling over that moral paradox. Either he didn't see it (which was doubtful) or he had decided to ignore it (which wasn't exactly like him either), or he was simply demonstrating a theory I'd been tendering for years, which was that there need not necessarily be any correlation between a man's actions and what he understands, even fully accepts, to be true. This apparent contradiction is a contradiction only in terms of the language of logic, and not in terms of the language of a man's acts. Whatever the case, Faber was one of the few men I have ever met who would fully accept, without any fancy moral foot-work, the wrongness of his acts, yet see no necessity whatsoever to justify, change or curtail them. "Yes, I commit unacceptable deeds," he said to me on another occasion. "That's simply what I do. I am as fully responsible for my actions as any man."

116

About a week before Faber's release date we were kneeling beside his chain saw on the mudflats trying to repair a faulty plug wire, and I asked him about his future plans. "Nothing in particular, really," he grunted, not looking up from his work at first and then, sitting up and grinning slightly abashed as he said: "But you know—and this'll sound a bit dumb, but what the hell—for the last three weeks I've repeatedly caught myself thinking about popcorn; like they sell in the theaters, you know? Haven't had any of that for over a year and a half now, ever since I was thrown into remand, and I've developed a real craving for some. So I think the first thing I'll do when they spring me is to head straight for the nearest popcorn place and gorge myself on about three cartonsful. Do you, incidentally, happen to know where the closest popcorn stand or theater is in this area?"

I wasn't exactly sure, but I was delighted to find that Faber had at least one unusual compulsion to his name and I promised to find out. During the next three days I checked and the idea caught on; soon half the camp was busily debating the pros and cons of various locations and routes; we smuggled in maps and the Theatre Section of the local Yellow Pages, and compared the personal testimonies of locally based inmates. Finally it was decided that the Stardust Theatre in Haney, although slightly farther away than the Ruskin Drive-In in Maple Ridge, was the preferred popcorn source, since the drive-in was only in business irregularly throughout the year, and it would never do, after eighteen months of waiting, to end up disappointed before a barred and empty concession stand. Besides, various connoisseurs insisted that the Stardust's popcorn had that certain *je ne sais quoi* which raised it well above the Ruskin stuff. So it was settled.

The night before his release we all wished Faber the very best, doused him thoroughly with water, as was the camp custom, shook cornflakes into his bed, as was somebody's independent childishness and saw him off, content that we were sending him into the world armed with nothing but the very best in maps and advice. We never did find out whether his popcorn quest ended in triumph or distress. Three months later, however, we heard that he was in the clink again, facing an absurdly long list of charges, which included half a dozen break-ins, one bank hold-up and the sale of a large amount of heroin to a narcotics officer . . .

FRAGMENT

33

I conducted a Creative Writing Workshop at Stave Lake Camp which involved about nineteen inmates, generally six or seven at a time. We met in one of the participants' huts each Sunday evening at eight-thirty to compare our weekly efforts. Only one other inmate had ever tried his hand at contemplative writing before, so most were equally innocent of the art and it was for me a very unusual learning experience to watch half a dozen relatively inarticulate men take pen in hand to try to explain themselves in a way that precluded threats or violence.

In fact, there developed in this respect a curious phenomenon around camp; whereas (for example) at any given fist fight, two opponents fought and thirty spectators milled about shouting encouragement, the new arrangement tended to have two opponents at each other's throats, twenty-five spectators shouting encouragement and five others busily scribbling into their notebooks. During lunch break or after supper as well, it became more and more common to see an inmate perched on a dump-truck seat, a fallen log or the stairs in front of his hut, scratching into a notebook or onto prison letterhead. Some of them began to explain themselves amazingly well in a very short time:

INTERIOR INDUSTRY

A falling tree
Crashes to earth in my mind,
I smile sadly
As branches bend
And snap
The echo dies away,
And solemn voices
Discuss which one
Must fall next ...

by D.D.

Or:

BULL SESSION

Stale cigar smoke
And
The air so thick
With words,
Of bravado
Men comparing scars

One, with none
Sits quietly
Despondent
Not too sure
If he's a man
Yet
Till the talk turns
To women
And he knows he must be
For he's had
One of those ...

by B.H.

Our workshop enthusiasm resulted in more than a few curious incidents, but the one I remember most vividly involved our loader-operator Harker. He was one of the most prolific writers in the group and probably the most persistent; when a line or stanza resisted him he kept after it with such dogged tenacity, he often ended up with half a dozen totally different poems from a single line. On this occasion he had just read a poem to the Sunday night workshop, which had turned its thumbs down on it, the consensus being (in the words of one of our more forceful participants) "I mean, like, the last stanza's completely fucked, man!" Being disinclined to argue unnecessarily with such pointed criticism, Harker took to his mattress and tried again; the result, in the workshop's estimation, paralleled the first disaster and Harker withdrew once more. By the time lights went out at 11:00 P.M. he'd practically worn out the corridor between our two rooms, but the stanza proved perverse, unruly, and he finally postponed further attempts until the following morning.

That had him up earlier than usual, greasing his huge machine and frowning purposefully to himself. The preoccupation with the uncooperative poem was obviously undiminished and we tussled with it for a bit, just to warm up. Then he climbed over one enormous water-filled tire (those machines are so heavy, they'd bounce three feet off the ground if they were bedded on air-filled tubes), threw the rig into gear and let go. Massive howling from the diesel, the braided treads tore at the ground, and when the diesel smoke had cleared Harker was already at the turn-off, heading for the lake. Old Fred Turner, the yard mechanic, once told me those beasts cost about twenty dollars a mile to run; even a flat tire on them costs about forty-five dollars to fix.

After that all was quiet for a while; the crew was in the bush bucking logs and I was busy in the toolshed learning how to rebuild chain saws (I'd been assigned to the job after Belaire left). About an hour passed. I had just walked out of the shed to test a rebuilt carburetor when I became aware of a faint but distinct humming, gradually increasing from the north. I stopped and listened harder; the sound was definitely moving down the logging road toward camp, but irregularly, widening now and then as it reached clearings. The roads in this area were lined with tall, inward-arching trees that funneled sound along their corridors like water sluicing along a sewer pipe. The road from camp, before it right-angled down to the lake, was in effect a huge quarter-mile-long tunnel, darkly green and flexing.

The humming had become a healthy growl. I could hear it clearly now and recognized it: it was the diesel roar of Harker's unmuffled loader.

And then it burst into the end of the tunnel, its huge front jaws bouncing and clanking, the rear end fishtailing slightly, bounding toward camp like a berserk rhinoceros, the roar of the engine pouring down the tube, overwhelming the camp in great gusts. He was down by the first gas tanks before I could even make out his hard hat in the operator's cage, a faint red blotch swimming about in the exhaust smoke.

The immense machine hurled into the yard in a magnificent arc around the pumps, dirt and gravel spraying in a beautifully fanned spume. Harker was out of the driver's seat even before the rig had completely stopped.

"I say, sire, pull yon monkey wrench out of your ear and feast yourself on damned deathless poetry!" he crowed, waving a shred of white paper gleefully under my nose. "Wrote the bloody thing right after I got out to the work site."

It was the last stanza of the poem, totally rewritten and, at a brief glance, quite successfully done.

"Told the bull I was working out how many loads I could get out of that gravel pit," he chortled. "First excuse that popped into my head."

"How the hell d'you get him to let you bring that monster all the way back to camp?"

122

Harker smirked and pulled gravely on his ear.

"Oh that. Yeah, I suppose that could be a problem. Didn't actually tell him anything about that, is what I didn't do. Hm. What d'you think I should say to the old coot?"

I found myself grinning from ear to ear, impressed. "Harker, you're a preposterous fucking maniac! Tell him you went into labor, hiccups every thirty seconds. Jesus. You mean you just up and buggered off with this thing?"

"Well, I had to show you the hootin thing while it was still hot, for godsake; if it hadn't been any good I'd have had to spend the afternoon working on it too, and I had to know what my schedule was going to be. I mean, it stands to reason, doesn't it?"

"I repeat my diagnosis: totally fried brain cells. Christ. Get this heap out of here and I'll say we fixed a leaky hydraulic hose. Here, I'll pour some fluid on the wrench, make it look downright Emile Zola."

Harker was already back in the seat. Diesel uproar. "Toodle-loo!" he hollered over the din. "Have a free bowel movement on me! Practice personal hygiene often!"

A vicious kick at the gear lever and the movie spooled itself off in reverse; I hunched behind a spotlight post to escape the flying dirt and gravel. After he was gone I sat down and, just for the hell of it, made some quick calculations with respect to miles, maintenance, time, current fuel costs, and so forth. According to my figures that stanza had cost the Corrections Service about two hundred and eighty-five dollars, give or take a ten-dollar bill.

Not bad, I had to admit. Not bad at all. Hopeful.

34

The Writing Workshop became a mainstay in my prison life, and, I think it true to assume, also in the lives of many of its members. It was an unexpected idea to the prison administrators at first, and an initially peculiar idea to the inmates as well, but the notion caught on and once it had become established, began to flourish briskly. At one stage, over a third of the camp population regularly crowded into somebody's room on Sunday nights to contribute or simply listen to the workshop session, and the amount of prose and poetry produced soon ran into the hundreds of pages. A number of inmates began to keep regular journals, and one in particular, Dennis Coleman, produced a four-hundred-page manuscript before he was released.

Coleman, in fact, was a good example of the initially almost illiterate prisoner facing himself nervously across an empty page. "I don't know what to say," he kept worrying when we discussed his writing plans. "When I sit down to put things on paper, I just clam up and my mind goes blank. I can't think of a thing to put down."

"Well, just begin by writing a page a day," I suggested. "And don't worry about being profound or impressive. Just write down what happened during the day point for point; treat the whole thing as if you were writing a laundry list."

That got him started, and once the page began to fill with words he became more relaxed about filling it with more. His first efforts naturally *did* read like laundry lists, but they got better quickly. From an initial pageful of:

"— got out of bed at 10:00 A.M. (Saturday: no work), got dressed & went for breakfast.

—came back to room & layed down for a short while & thought about todays plans.

—decided to work on the slab of wood I got out of the bush yesterday, went to where it was stored and discovered it was missing—very pissed off.

—came back to my bed and tryed to think of something else to do to keep my mind busy—decided to make a sling-shot—didn't work so well but had to get my mind off the time dragging.

—wandered over to watch T.V.—nothing on that intrest me so I came back to room and layed down & dozed off for a couple of hours . . ."

he began to steadily reduce the number of incidents described but kept up the page length, forcing himself to consider the day's events in more and more detail and depth. Soon he was managing:

"One thing I have noticed in this camp is how some peoples personalities change like day into night. Terry for instance was when I first arrived here, a very friendly understanding person. It didn't take long at all for us to become friends. We always worked together, and after work constructed or cut someone down for laughs together (such as the camp dummy). Slowly the months pass by and I have noticed an extreme

change in him and I believe that everyone including the guards have also. He has changed from a considerate, easy-going person to an inconsiderate, rebellious person. This doesn't mean he doesn't have good days, he does, but very seldom. If he wakes up happy he's usually bitchy by noon for the rest of the day. If he wakes up bitchy he's usually happy and joking around for the rest of the day. Some people don't even like to talk to him anymore, for they are fearful of how he might react to what is said. Sometimes he'll take a joke and another time he will take things serious and start threatening. This is mainly the reason why I have stopped, to a certain extant, associating with him. Many other inmates are doing the same, except the ones who appear to be afraid to contrdict him. I sometimes wonder how many friends he'd have if there weren't new people coming in and out of here."

Finally, by the time he was approaching his release date, he had become quite adept at plotting himself, writing more and more introspective pieces as he learned to think an idea through to its conclusion and to evaluate it:

"Time is running somewhat short for me now; with only 53 more days to go, I'm beginning to notice time passing much more slowly. I don't like it at all. I am aware of the fact that once a prisoner starts noticing time going by, he begins to shake it rough. This worries me; I'm starting to catch myself thinking of the Outside much more than usual. I find myself wondering whether or not I will go directly to work or school. I sometimes picture myself sitting in a classroom or even working in a gas station; I still haven't made up my mind which one I'd like to do. I'd like to be in a classroom, but then I would also like to be making money. After working here for 30¢ a day, I think even $3.00 an hour will feel good and satisfying for awhile. I find myself daydreaming quite a lot lately. It distracts me while I'm trying to do my work and causes me to lose interest in it, which tends to make the day *drag a lot. When the day drags, I usually feel much more quick-tempered and crabby. I also seem to be having a much harder time too, and I never seem to get a complete night's sleep. In the morning I can never remember what it was that I dreamt; I only know I wake up often, almost every night. These are the standard symptoms of shaking rough time, and somehow I have to learn to ignore the fact that my time is getting short. That's what is bringing this on."*

Others didn't begin under quite such a formidable handicap, but their progress was no less impressive. There was a young Indian prisoner, Larry Commodore, who began by writing more or less passable poetry, then suddenly found his voice and positively shot ahead, composing verse with a sureness and maturity that never failed to baffle me. His early work might be demonstrated by this untitled poem:

> *"a smooth flat stone*
> *no larger than a child's fist*
> *is thrown by the young man standing on the beach*
>
> *the stone skips across the water twice*
>
> *then is caught by the water*
> *and sinks*
>
> *the young man gazes at the slightly disturbed water*
> *the last strand of yellow sunlight*
> *glances off the water*
> *the young man turns and is silhouetted by the sunset*
> *the water is a tarnished yellow mirror*
> *the young man's bare feet sink into the sand . . ."*

Three months later he handed me this excerpt, which eventually became part of a much longer poem he entitled *Red Elegies*, and which was recorded for CBC Radio's "Sunday Supplement":

"Carl Sandburg, the tears have made furrows in that weary
face of yours
and the years have left wrinkles and
white hair
and a defensive yet piercing stare
like a lion staring at the barrel of a rifle,

Carl Sandburg, the day is cold and rain is falling
I've stood at this window an hour
and studied the dark cold land
your words echo and fade

Carl Sandburg, what wisdom is there now
six feet underground
and in the dead pages of books
what words would take this day
and turn it into sunshine
what words
would echo and shatter
the desolation of this land
what words
would soothe the soul of this young Indian
who dreams of changes
who has seen death

Carl Sandburg, the day is fast fading,
there are horsemen milling about in the distance
there is talk of apocalypse . . ."

All in all, we had a terrific time in that workshop. One of
the most common complexes among inmates is the feeling that
all their lives they have been told they have nothing to say or
that nothing they might have to say is worth saying. The
workshop demonstrated that this was not at all the case, that
they did have all kinds of things to say and that they were
quite capable of learning how to say them, and very aptly at
that. I found this, in fact, to be another area of major failing

128

in prisons: it seems never to have occurred to anyone to try to rehabilitate inmates by teaching them simple confidence in themselves, which is an enormous source of power. Instead, prisons conspire to make an inmate believe he's simply an animal, a failure and a derelict, then act surprised when he obliges them by becoming just that. The workshop "experiment" demonstrated that the confidence approach has a far higher potential for success.

Of the inmates who participated in it, for example, Larry Commodore is now enrolled in university courses at a regional college, loader-operator Harker worked for a year in outlying (high-paying) bush camp road-building operations and is now developing real estate in Quesnel with his earnings. Bob Kleiner, who hadn't held a job for more than a day at a time in his life, took a semi-trailer truck-driving course and has now formed his own trucking firm, carrying long-haul freight across Canada in two huge trucks which he's paying off at an accelerated rate. Coleman, on the other hand, is back in jail, but he was a heroin addict who hadn't kicked the habit, so until the laws change on that score his reincarceration was a foregone conclusion.

The Writing Workshop experiment was actually the brain-child of Marnie Knechtel of the Prison Arts Foundation (Brantford, Ontario) who contacted me after my arrest and asked if I'd be interested in putting such an idea into practice once my sentence had begun. They'd been simmering the idea for some time, she said, and had simply been waiting for the right moment to put it into effect. That "right moment" came when they heard that a writer was being sentenced to a prison term in British Columbia, where she also happened to know the Deputy Minister of Corrections and would therefore be able to get administrative clearance for such a project. I agreed give it a try, and once I got to Stave Lake began the workshop informally while letters passed back and forth between wardens and ministers until clearance was obtained.

Once everything was formalized I managed to convince the Deputy Warden that we needed a much better library to back up our workshop activity than the few pulp novels Stave Lake had. As a result, I was driven home under guard and permitted to plunder my own extensive library, bringing back half a dozen large boxes of books. They were stored in my room and made available to all prison camp inmates, marking the first time anybody had ever been able to get his hands on a good book at Stave Lake Camp. The trade in these books, incidentally, was brisk and extensive; over a third of them were always out on loan at any given time.

There were other advantages I gained from the workshop. Since the huts were noisy and the rooms very small, I got the camp officers to allow me to use the First-Aid Room for writing and editing purposes, and it was there that I eventually installed the old Underwood, which I used intermittently for the writing of production reports for the Deputy Warden. As a result I was finally able to start writing this book, for which I had previously only been able to make hasty notations in several scribblers, since the huts were impossible places in which to concentrate, let alone write. The First-Aid Room, however, was situated in a set of construction trailers not attached to the huts, making it a relatively quiet place to work, and that's where I increasingly set up shop as the months went by. Eventually, the First-Aid Room was the first place people looked for me when they wanted me for anything.

At first, of course, there was considerable resistance to the whole idea of my writing and typing; for inmates, it was unprecedented, too "administrative-looking" and too arrogant; for guards it was similarly unprecedented and arrogant, but also potentially dangerous inasmuch as they immediately came to the conclusion I might be writing some sort of exotic exposé. The inmates relaxed considerably when I began my practice of composing parole applications and temporary absence requests, and the guards simply had to get used to seeing me behind a typewriter since I could always say I was working on the Deputy Warden's material. In time, however, I became something like a basic Camp Resource, and eventually even guards began to bring me forms and nonconfidential reports to compose or type.

FRAGMENT

35

It's ten o'clock at night; the truck has just returned from Visits and we're crowded into my room now, eight or nine of us on the bunks and stools, all of us talking in low, almost conspiratorial voices, no one wanting to break it off just yet, no one wanting to fully snap back into prison for just a few more moments; for another hour we're still somehow different from the others, still slightly altered by that brief exposure to Outside air, still too full of the suddenly revived longings for wives, mistresses, families; still too churned up by the good news and the bad news, the no news where we expected to find at least something, the latest troubles we're once again so infuriatingly helpless to do anything about, the unexpected (well, maybe not so unexpected), maybe imagined (maybe not) coolness of yet another lover getting tired of the strain (and what about us, goddammit, what about us!). We sit here in this curious huddle, and for a short while our defenses are remarkably down, the toughness and the bristle; it's like a brief cease-fire during which we don't have to bother with the strutting, the cockiness, the macho routines because we've

132

just seen each other hungry and anxious with friends and lovers and we're all still a bit embarrassed about that, but it seems to be all right.

For another hour we'll talk recklessly and longingly about the past, the future, unpack some of these gentle, absurd recollections every inmate keeps hidden for the most difficult times, and I'm astonished again at the sudden humanity and warmth everyone is capable of when he thinks it's safe to display. Frenchie tells thoughtfully about his wife, about how they made love once in an open field somewhere and how it wasn't so good because they were both really nervous about being so out in the open, but it was nice anyway, sort of. And Bernie says yeah, it's kinda weird, isn't it, how girls kind of cry pretty easy at times like that and it makes you all confused 'cause you don't have a clue what to say, like, and you don't even know what to feel sometimes when that happens except kind of weird. What makes them do that anyway, do we think? And Frenchie thinks it's probably because they don't know what to feel right then themselves; they just maybe cry because that's what women do a lot. It's all that weird chemistry inside them changing all the time; a lot of the time it really mixes up all their feelings, you know.

Hell, Davis says; his girl friend doesn't cry much at all; she throws stuff a lot though. Man, you oughta see her go. Whew. Her parents are Presbyterian, actually. Man, was she pissed off when he got busted. Oh boy. Was that the one who was visiting him tonight? Frenchie wants to know; the one with the blue coat and the hair up like that? Yeah, that was her. Pretty nice, real nice, Frenchie says generously, and we all murmur agreement. And then we sit for a while longer, pondering the mysteries of women and drifting with the memories they bring to mind.

Later we try to make Gryphon feel better because his father came to see him again, and his father just can't seem to lay off the sermons; he's still giving Gryphon royal shit for

133

something that happened almost two years ago, and he just won't stop. He's already screwed up Gryphon's parole application twice—keeps saying, "You just cool your ass off in there for a while, son, until you learn a little sense." That sounds so incredible to us we can't even believe it; how anyone, especially your own family, could refuse to help you get out of this hole.

But then there was Harris's mother, remember fat Harris from the kitchen? Well, his mother actually *wrote* to the Warden and told him not to let her son out because he'd just start smoking marijuana again anyway. That sounds even more than incredible; in fact, that goes far beyond any family loyalties we're honoring tonight and Bernie suggests somebody oughta burn that cunt's house down or something, with her in it like, and that sounds pretty appropriate to us all. Jesus. They just don't know what it's like in here; that's the trouble with all them people out there, they don't know the first damn thing they're talking about when they just say toss 'em in the clink. Shit, it's easy for *them* to say; they don't have to do the time. They don't have to live half the rest of their lives in goddamn tunnels!

We all nod and make agreeing noises although we don't really want to get into that; that's standard jail talk and the sort of thing we can kick around any time. Right now we're trying to linger a bit longer in that warm after-Visits bath in which nobody's inclined to blackmail anybody because everybody's got something to lose . . . not that we're not all aware of what's bothering Bernie. The police have sent in a report that his girl friend's on junk again, and now the Review Board won't even consider his application until she's clean. Of which there isn't much hope, of course. . . .

FRAGMENT

36

It's unquestionably a mixed blessing, this business of visits. Visits probably cost an inmate three times as much as they're worth; a single one-hour visit is often enough to throw a man into a frenzy for a week; a regular weekly visit can keep an inmate unsettled through his entire term. Nevertheless I've rarely met an inmate who would turn down a visit if it was offered, and many use up their entire mail ration (two letters a week) to arrange for them as often as they can. I'm sure I do much harder time as a result of my own visits, but I don't suppose I'd give them up any more readily than an addict would give up a fix.

The trouble with visits is that they won't let you forget. The more alive you keep your memories of the Street, the worse things look and feel to you Inside. The less you know about what you're missing on the Street, the easier it is to imagine you're not missing anything at all. In order to shake easy time Inside you have to rid yourself of all Outside voices, Outside problems (which you can't resolve in any case) and Outside comparisons with Inside life. The sooner you give up trying

135

to live your life in two places at once, the sooner your time eases into that long, mindless lope which makes a year only marginally longer than six months, a fin only slightly more drawn out than a deuce. It's a phenomenon well known to old-timers and lifers, who count on it to get them through sentences that would otherwise probably drive them right into the ground. Visits, however, tend to interfere with all that.

It's probably safe to say that in 80 percent of all cases it's a man's Outside life that, directly or indirectly, gets him into trouble Inside. Often it's just the little things, the harmless gossip his wife might prattle away, trying to fill the two hours during which they sit stiffly side by side under a guard's gaze, wanting desperately to do everything else but talk. She may mention difficulties with the rent or the baby, with neighbors or family, with bureaucrats, car insurance or sleepless nights. She might be feeling badly that day and seem cold or remote, or she might even be drunk or stoned or simply have given up that week, wanting him to hold *her* up for a change—it can be anything at all. And in an atmosphere tense with the sense that two weeks or two months of the past have to lived up-to-date in two hours, the opportunities for misunderstandings are myriad. I won't even try to remember how many of my nights after visits have been spent penning long, apologetic letters to my girl friend trying to explain my clumsy behavior to her, her perplexing behavior to me and our duplex confusions together. No matter how hard we try, it is almost impossible to relate to each other normally.

And yet each week without fail I grow impatient as visit day approaches, the whole camp begins to tense as everyone waits, each inmate hoping anxiously that this time he'll be on the Visit List, that his name will crackle through that fat gray walkie-talkie the guard packs like a hand gun on his belt. At Stave Lake, visits are a particularly complex ritual since the camp lies far too deep in the bush for visitors to come to it themselves; instead, inmates are trucked all the way in to the

Haney Correctional Centre, where the Visiting Lounge is set aside for us from 7:30–9:00 P.M. To get there in time, those with visits must be let off work an hour early to shower and change, and the names of such inmates are radioed to the guards at the work sites to signal their release. Those not listed, on the other hand, must work on until quitting time, an hour and a half later.

A cell mate who rarely got visits once noted bitterly: "Yeah, it's great, really great. You can't imagine how unspeakably galling it is to watch all those delighted faces piling into that truck, then to turn back to your shovel feeling you're being punished with extra work because nobody out there gives enough of a shit about you to come see you once in a while . . ."

Back at camp, however, the excitement virtually shimmers in the air, showers burst into action, inmates sing and yodel short bursts of song (Visits being the only occasion on which one's fellow inmates will stand for that sort of thing inasmuch as they're feeling the same way), cavorting about like high-spirited colts; it's a time of renewed and giddy hopes, with the difficulties of last time willfully forgotten once again. Visits also constitute one of the rare times an inmate is permitted to wear his own casual clothes (if he has any), giving him back at least a little of his individuality for a few hours.

At six o'clock the truck pulls out for Haney and at seven o'clock it arrives, off-loading us at a side entrance where we're marched into a holding cell until somebody can get around to searching us. We sit on the concrete floor or stare restlessly through the bars, exchanging shouts with other inmates passing by or nervously flexing hands and knees since there's no room to walk it off. Eventually we're cleared for the Lounge and a second steel door slides aside to let us in. The whole crews spills through as fast as it can, laying claim to the small groupings of tables and chairs first-come first-served until all are filled. Then we sit and wait.

The wait itself is almost enough to drive you frantic.

137

Everyone stares anxiously through the window to the parking lot, watching for familiar cars or faces, and when the first of the visitors come, the disappointment on the faces of those to whom they don't belong would be comic to watch if you weren't so busy being disappointed yourself. As the precious minutes tick away you become angry, then furious at such indefensible waste, a growing rage spreading and deepening through your chest until you're convinced the first thing you'll do the minute that inconsiderate little bitch walks through the door is to bust . . . And then suddenly she's there, grinning anxiously at you through the glass, and that rage vanishes as if it never existed while you ecstatically use up one of your two embraces (sign posted on the Lounge bulletin board: *Inmates will be permitted a single embrace upon greeting their visits, and one upon departing. No other intimacies will be allowed.*), then steer past those others who are still being enraged and disappointed and sit down at your little table in the corner . . .

Maybe it goes well, maybe it doesn't. Whatever happens, an hour and a half later they signal Visit's End and the visitors flock back down the hill through the Main Gate into the parking lot; we all stand at the window watching their diminishing backs. Nobody says much of anything. The trip back in the truck is always much more restrained, nothing at all like the rambunctious horseplay of the trip in. Inmates sit lost in thought or talk quietly, maybe handing around a pack of cigars or some chocolate bars they've received (if the right guard was on) as a gift. When we arrive back at camp it's already dark; the perimeter searchlights highlight the prison like a factory on night shift. Here and there inmates slip through the lights and shadows, passing from building to building. We melt away into the dark as well, some possibly regathering without formal arrangement in somebody's room if they feel thusly driven, others drifting about just avoiding people, trying to come to terms with whatever the evening has churned up inside them.

138

For the rest of that evening, and possibly for the next whole week, the shock waves from that Visit Night will be visible in varying degrees throughout the inmate population. The next day, at work, you can pick out those who have had bad visits almost as easily as if they'd been painted green; a prisoner doggedly working away with that deep inward look, occasionally forgetting to raise his axe again at the end of a downward swing until he's snapped out of his reverie by a guard's angry shout; a normally cooperative inmate suddenly sullen and testy, picking fights with his cell mates or sitting as far away from them at lunch as the guard will permit, brooding; a generally well-coordinated prisoner suddenly unusually accident-prone, inclining to axe cuts or chain-saw slashes, headlong falls or cracked shins . . . And sometimes, after two or three days of this, or even weeks, the sudden break—in the morning at wake-up the man is gone, out past the night guards and into the bush, trying to make it out to the highway to hitch a ride home. Because that's where the police find them nine times out of ten. And if they've been lucky, they've managed to straighten out whatever domestic anxieties were preying on their minds (even if it was only a reassuring couple of hours making love to their girl friends or wives); if not, they've only added to their troubles. In any case, they've increased their own sentences by anywhere from three to six extra months for escaping from legal custody, which they'll have to do back in the cells; escaped prison camp inmates are almost always returned to maximum security to finish off the rest of their time behind bars.

But visits are only one way in which a man's Outside life can reach Inside to jab and worry him; letters are another, often equally potent, agent. To the best of my knowledge, every prison in Canada censors prisoners' mail for this reason (and also others). "Dear John" letters, letters announcing family tragedies or even just angry outbursts from wives or lovers are one of the most effective ways to snap an inmate's already overtightened emotional mainspring. The number of prison breaks resulting from disturbing mail accounts for by far the largest proportion of the so-called "impulsive escapes."

At Stave Lake (an "innovative" camp with a record to protect) the policy to forestall such outbreaks ("negative statistics") is similar to its pragmatic if somewhat insensitive strategy with respect to inmate fights (see Fragment 30). If an inmate receives an unsettling letter and is considered insufficiently stable to handle it, he's simply sent back to the cells for a few days or weeks to "wear it off," after which he may or may not come back, depending very much on the whims of fate (as the Administration is sometimes called). In other words, at a time when a man most needs a bit of sympathy, when he's been hit with one of the worst cudgels the Outside can bring down on his head (e.g., his wife has left him, his child has died, etc.) they grab him and shove him back into the cages—"for his own good," of course. And I will admit that this method doubtlessly lowers the prison's impulsive-escape record, although I also strongly suspect that such credits invariably turn up as debits elsewhere on the balance sheet, where they may be less publicly visible but where they're no doubt far more serious in their implications.

In my own case, I eventually had to stop answering all my letters, and in the end even stopped paying very close attention to their actual contents. Not that my Outside affairs were in any particular disarray; it was just that it became too emotionally exhausting to switch so constantly from hot to cold, to live completely Inside while considering Outside matters sufficiently to be able to speak intelligently about them to the people who lived there. There was also, of course, the fact that you could never really say what you wanted to say, what with the censors constantly scouring your letters for evidence of emotional instability. I suspect that had I been entirely frank with anyone about my situation, I'd have done most of my time in Haney Correctional. Of course I did manage to smuggle out the odd letter to a few very close friends, just to keep them up-to-date on the true state of affairs, but most were written with the censor as much in mind as the people to whom they were addressed, effectively making them useless as real information and reducing them, for all intents and purposes, to a wave of the hand through the ferns.

On the other hand, I was damned grateful for every letter I got in that it kept my sense of security intact—each letter a kind of signal telling me somebody out there was keeping me in mind. There's really no way to exaggerate the value of that kind of signal—I sometimes got the impression that if *Reader's Digest* were to send one of those "personalized" mass-produced letters to every inmate in the prison assuring him that HE had been chosen to receive some idiotic gift because *Reader's Digest* valued HIM as a beloved customer, the place would positively glow with pleasure and relief that someone somewhere Out There actually gave a damn.

FRAGMENT

37

After four months in prison they gave me a weekend out. I hadn't felt in such turmoil since I was a child, when I seem to recall feeling fear or happiness far more intensely than after my teens. It took an entire day to be cleared through the Haney Correctional Centre's labyrinth of offices, checkpoints and gates. When I finally passed through the last, the Main Gate, it was almost evening and half my weekend had already evaporated. She was waiting in the parking lot in the dented little Japanese car she drove, asleep. She'd been there for seven hours.

I was so tense, I just stood there for a while, watching her breathing. This world outside the gates had become so unfamiliar, some idiot part of me just wanted to walk back in and escape the emotional furor involved in dealing with it. By Sunday noon it had abated only slightly; we were sitting in a small Greek restaurant on Twelfth Avenue, and I was still having difficulty suppressing the urge to counterattack when somebody reached too abruptly for the salt. These people all around me, carelessly laughing, thoughtlessly waving their arms about and casually leaving their backs exposed, had become complete strangers; they reeked of freedom and paid absolutely no attention to it. Somehow, I can't say exactly how, the entire scene seemed dangerous, as if a crowd of children were playing ball with live hand grenades.

I couldn't snap out of it. In one way or another, everything I encountered became simply an extension of prison; the only thing that came to mind at the sight of the superbly prepared salad was that it wasn't like the cabbage we ate Inside. Between silences, I talked of prison life until I realized I was surrounding myself with it, then subsided. Finally we gave it up, walked back to the house and made love slowly, wordlessly, until it was time to go.

It was as close as I got to "being out." On the way back I was already so busy thinking ahead about how to negotiate the upcoming bureaucratic hurdles that the ride became tedious and I wished it were over more quickly. I said my goodbyes hurriedly in the parking lot and hastened through the Main Gate to join a knot of other inmates who had also returned from similar leaves. It was like a fraternity reunion, and we didn't even know each other. When I reached the main courtyard, which first affords a complete view of the whole prison complex, I suddenly realized with a mixture of embarrassment and dismay that for the first time in thirty-six hours I felt relaxed and back in my skin, and that the bastards had caught me too, goddamn them, and I hadn't even felt the net come down.

38

When I returned from my first weekend pass a few days ago I found that Cal Winterfield, the baker, was in serious trouble; he was in the Hole, stripped of his pass privileges and about to be sent back to maximum security. Oakalla. He had attacked two members of the kitchen staff with a knife, been drawn off by a guard wielding a chunk of firewood and been finally subdued by staff reinforcements, who had then dragged him into the tool hut and closed the door. When they emerged a quarter of an hour later, Winterfield was hauled to the hospital and then to Solitary while the guards stood around in the office pouring iodine over their knuckles. As is usual after such incidents, an uneasy lull settled over the camp, the inmates speaking only in low voices, guards and inmates uncomfortably or sullenly avoiding one another's glances, and all privileges or nonregulation "arrangements" between staff and the inmate body suddenly adrift in uncertain limbo.

The Winterfield incident, while hardly different from numberless similar misadventures, affected me more than most because I had known the man well and liked him; he was generally easy to work around and had a sturdy sense of humor. But he also had something else, at first glance a mere temper problem which it was wise to keep in mind; at considerable intervals he would suddenly blow in all directions, quite indiscriminately and wildly though mostly harmlessly, if one had the sense to stay out of his way.

I said "at first glance" because eventually I came to recognize him as one of a strange breed of inmate I kept running into and marveling at; men who seemed to be bent singlemindedly on their own destruction, living as though by the instincts of lemmings. Demonstrations of this occurred randomly as a rule, but most dramatically just before such men were about to be released. During that time most inmates tend to toe the line more fastidiously, giving wide berth to obvious trouble and pulling instinctively back from any plans to perpetrate it. Even those with much of their sentence left to serve cooperate in this, automatically releasing short-timers from obligations that might blot their records and thus interfere with their release. Typically, it was precisely at such a time in his own sentence that Winterfield began to complain noisily about lunchtime sandwiches, sandwiches that had been, to my recollection, consistently bad from the day I arrived. There was little logical reason why he should have picked such a crucial time to become a gourmet critic.

But there was more; within a period of six days he was cited in three scraps with other inmates, one of which was serious enough to send his opponent to hospital. It was only that man's insistent declaration that a fall had caused the injury that saved Winterfield—and the other man as well, of course. A break-in into the Storage Hut failed when the paper clip he was using broke off in the lock, setting off a full investigation from which he was saved only by the rigid prisoners' code of "us against them at all costs," no matter who has done what and what you might know about it.

Finally, as if totally exasperated with his own dogged luck, he grabbed a knife from the kitchen and attacked the two pot washers whose responsibility it was to prepare the sandwiches; that act was unequivocal and couldn't be ignored—nor, I'm convinced, was it intended to be.

It wasn't only that Winterfield was afraid to leave prison and face the Outside—this was no doubt also true, but that made him no different from virtually half the prison population—it was something more than that, rather an unmistakable self-hatred set ablaze at varying intervals, often for no apparent reason and often against all reason entirely, about-facing him from an already opening gate or long-awaited reclassification and hurling him back at his captors kicking and slashing, back, back past parole considerations, back down through all the levels of the cages, all the security clearances, the whole prison fish ladder, back even past the ludicrous psychologists' interviews and the Classifications monkeys, the fingerprinters, the picture-takers—back finally to the very last wall, to be handcuffed and frog-marched off to the Hole and its iron cot, having undone in ten minutes what it took months, often years, to attain. Back to the very beginning, dazed, shaken up, suddenly aware of what has happened and instinctively recognizing it, hating himself for that insidious treason within and probably sensing far back in his mind that it will happen this way again (and again), and that each time he will advance a shorter distance toward Release than he managed the time before. . . .

Solitary: The Hole. A dimly lit corridor flanked by two rows of metal cages, those on one side open-barred, the others completely enclosed in steel plate with only a small peephole in the door. The enclosed cells have their ceilings fitted with countersunk shower heads and their floors with drains; when a prisoner "loses it" and begins to shout and pound on the door (it's pitch black in there) an attendant douses him with a burst of water. Sometimes the drains are plugged and the water seeps out under the door; the sight of it is somehow irrationally unnerving, as if it were a seepage of blood. The dark-tiled floor makes the water look oddly thick and black.

The steel-plated cages are empty; the prisoner sits all day on the freezing tiles. In the open-barred cages he has a choice: the tiles or a cot made of interlaced steel bands (no mattress from 6:00 A.M. to 11:00 P.M.). The bands are almost a quarter of an inch thick and cleverly spaced in such a manner that you can't possibly lie on them for more than a minute without their digging into various parts of your body, often pinching the nerves in your thighs or shoulders so that, should you fall asleep, you wake up completely numbed, unable to move your limbs. The first time it happened to me I almost panicked; I thought I'd been permanently paralyzed. It took a good ten minutes for my legs to thaw out.

I was thrown into the Hole for being party to the making of "home brew," a rather demure concoction of doubtful alcoholic content made from potato peelings, left-over fruit juice, left-over porridge, apples or apple cores, raisins, bread, coffee grounds and sugar, all pitched together into a plastic pail. The preparation is (so goes the recipe) left to ferment for seven days, then crudely strained through a pillow case. The resulting liquid is furtively downed in fast gulps in the soap-smelling laundry room since its powerful odor of garbage dump makes it a tricky liquid to be found in the vicinity of. After all conspirators have had their fill, the routine calls for everyone to get together in somebody's cell to convince each other that they are indeed drunk, after which all can go to bed secure in the belief that they have been. For the next several days the camp crackles and pops with breathless descriptions of the wild party held last Friday night in Hut Six.

When I arrived in Solitary I was lodged in one of the open-barred cages since my offense was of a minor nature. My clothes were taken away and replaced with an ill-fitting blue pajama, the bottom of which wouldn't stay up and clearly wasn't meant to. Absolutely nothing could be taken into the cages except a copy of the Bible—and the guard checked the cells regularly to make sure they weren't being used as pillows or mini-mattresses. Breakfast was a rubber egg and a slice of cold, sodden toast; lunch passed unheeded and supper was a paper plate covered with food. Those were the highlights of the day; there weren't any more.

I couldn't see any of the others in their cages but they were no doubt doing the same things as I; the possibilities were rather limited. I sat on the edge of my cot, stared at the ceiling, stared at the floor, tried lying on the steel bands, gave that up, lay on the floor, decided against that, resettled on the edge of the cot and stared at the ceiling and the floor. There was nothing. Nothing to see, nothing to hear, nothing to smell or do. The brain, idled and in neutral, fussed and balked in increasing frustration.

Eventually I began to marvel at the magnificent simplicity of it all; how with such minimal means they had managed to concoct an environment so very successfully uncomfortable. Had there been a mattress it would have been easy to drift away into old memories, mental doodles, or to become engrossed in the Bible. As it was, the physical discomfort interfered at every turn with the mind's attempts to concentrate; I couldn't read more than two verses without having to shift positions in the endless search for a comfortable posture. My back became criss-crossed with ridges and scores from attempts to lie on the cot. I started shivering and couldn't stop, and the dim light from the corridor, a flickering neon affair, began to give me headaches. All in all, I was eventually forced to realize that I was losing the battle and that a totally different response was called for.

Weighing all the possibilities, I decided the numbed limbs were the answer. I lay back across the steel bands and let them dig into the flesh until all feeling faded and the pain was gone, then cupped my hands under my head to protect it until the fingers went numb. After I'd had my eyes closed for several minutes I found myself drifting off into an odd cottony kind of coma that must have lasted at least five hours, ending when the guard clanged a piece of pipe against the bars to indicate supper. The clanging registered so suddenly that I jerked up and was already falling to the floor before I realized I couldn't move my arms and legs. Fortunately I hit the tiles buttocks first. The guard's face didn't change and he simply pushed my paper plate under the door; no doubt it wasn't an unfamiliar sight.

149

After that I came up with the idea of rebuilding my house. Just before being arrested I'd built myself a small house on a mountain in B.C.; now, to keep my mind working busily enough to ignore my body, I started the project all over again, making every cut, digging every hole, driving every nail, painting every board, reconstructing the entire building in my mind. It proved an engrossing undertaking, in the process of which I discovered several items I'd forgotten to complete in the real house, and several I decided I wanted changed. (One of the first things I did after my release was in fact to complete the unfinished carpentry I'd discovered in the Hole, also rebuilding the various items I'd changed my mind about at the time.)

When the guard finally opened my cage five days later to inform me that my time was up, he looked somewhat perplexed when I informed him as gravely as I could that I wasn't quite ready to come out yet; I still had to finish the front porch.

For a prisoner, of course, a guard is possibly the lowest imaginable form of humanoid life, a species somewhere about the level of the gorilla and often rather easily mistaken for one. He's called a bull, a pig, a wethead or a screw, and it's understood he'd rather shoot you than give you the time of day, stick you in the back rather than give you a crust of bread. Former prison guards (or police or narcotics officers) who have committed felonies and are sentenced to prison terms might as well roll over and play dead; they're done for anyway. The memory of the inmate body is astonishingly long.

The intriguing aspect of this view of guards, however, is that no inmate I've ever met came by it through his own experience—at least not initially. It's an opinion a prisoner automatically picks up at the door, along with his issue of prison clothes and his government-issue toothbrush, and from that point on he simply looks for incidents to *confirm* the view. Without even having to discuss it, he understands instinctively that such an opinion goes along with his khaki shirt and his cheapo boots, that it's wise to establish one's loyalties clearly and that guard-hating is an act which clearly confirms such a loyalty to the inmate cause. It's expressly part of the function of being a prisoner.

The unflattering guard profile is mostly untrue, but for an inmates there are, nevertheless, a number of signal advantages to subscribing to it. For one thing, the designation of a common enemy helps considerably to ensure inmate solidarity, which in turn tends to reduce the incidence rate of informers. For another, a vigorous hatred or anger is a remarkably dependable source of strength for an underdog; most inmates rely on it to carry them through the frustrations of imprisonment to a far greater extent than they can probably afford to realize. Because no matter how justified or unjustified our practice of imprisoning malefactors may be, it has always been true that everything in a human being revolts against being stuffed into a cage, and *that* becomes the major issue once he or she is behind bars, not (or very much less) the question of *why* he is there. A prisoner will play along with the rehabilitative gobbledygook he's fed Inside for obvious reasons, but what he really wants is simply to get the hell out of there, and the actions of the guards provide a handy outlet for his resentment and irritation at being unable to do so. In this peculiar way, the guard stands as buffer between an inmate's normal human exasperation and his all-out psychic explosion.

Unfortunately, however, there is also the matter of the truth contained in that old adage, "You treat a horse like a donkey long enough and he'll oblige by beginning to act like one." Most guards, unlike police officers or narcotics agents, never intended to become prison security personnel in the first place; for one thing, the pay is too low and the working conditions rather less than delightful. Most simply blundered into the job because they could find no other, and most are constantly on the lookout for better work somewhere else.

The qualifications for becoming a prison guard are so low as to be almost nonexistent, which doesn't exactly attract the brightest minds and the most highly motivated humanitarians. Many guards, in fact, are retired army (British or Canadian) personnel who tend to make little distinction between their old place of work and their new. But above all else, it is simply a fact that most guards didn't become guards in order to satisfy some latent sadism or other perversion in their characters; they simply answered all the want-ads and Corrections gave them a job.

Then, of course, the picture often *does* change, and the aforementioned adage comes into play. The new guard, initially naïve and uncertain about the ways of inmates and the prison, is soon taken advantage of by certain more experienced inmates and has his fingers burned once or twice. In retaliation he takes refuge behind the letter of the law and becomes, very quickly, an inflexible, unthinking automaton programmed by the directives and book of rules. That, needless to say, is bound to get him into difficulties sooner or later since the requirements of everyday life in prison (or anywhere) rarely dovetail neatly with the rigid maxims of a printed rulebook; and besides, when crossed, inmates aren't exactly famous for their unfailing courtesy and honeyed phrases.

There's only so much abuse a man will take before his ego begins to show the strain, and guards, for their part, aren't necessarily the most self-secure and stable specimens of the human race. Ergo, a battlefront develops, and each side digs in to defend its rights, its view and its self-esteem. Naturally, all the ancillary hack work comes into play, the propaganda, the accusations, even the occasional assault. Guards are of course already unionized, and more recently inmates have begun to unionize as well. As is typical of such situations, everybody stops thinking for himself and begins to speak and act simplistically along party lines, reducing everything to a question of black or white. Such states of affairs rarely bring out the best in people. Eventually, some guards *do* become what the inmates accuse them of, and some inmates *do* conform to the profile that security personnel draw of them.

There is, for example, a guard at Pine Ridge Camp who is an ignorant, loud-mouthed and temperamental bully, who treats inmates like scum and who carries on a full program of personal vendettas against inmates he has for his own peculiar reasons decided to dislike. He speaks only in snarls or sneers, orders prisoners about as if they were little better than dogs and is virtually impossible to reason with on almost any matter whatsoever. I tend normally to be a fairly even-tempered person, but that man often made my blood boil, and I could clearly see where the stereotype of guards as brutal, beer-bellied pugilists came from. Fortunately there aren't many like him in the system, and those guards who are inclined to be decent suffer more than they might realize through the actions of such a man.

The inmates, of course, have their parallel sinners, and I can remember a number of occasions when totally unprovoked hurls of abuse brought retaliations from guards that I considered totally justified. In one instance an inmate we'll call Rockford attempted to take more than his share of a tray full of carefully counted-out grilled cheese sandwiches; this would have left the last man in line with none. The guard calmly explained the logistics of the situation and ordered the inmate to put the extra sandwiches back. Rockford refused "because I'm hungry, ya goddamn fuckin pig!" and hurled the sandwiches into the mud. The guard promptly put Rockford on charge and had him sent back to the cells, which, in view of several similar incidents Rockford had perpetrated during the preceding months, seemed reasonable enough. Rockford, incidentally, was the inmate referred to in Fragment 21, who was nearly strung up in his cell during the Haney riots.

154

Between those extremes lie a thousand minor irritations, little flare-ups over a host of administrative squabbles—forms not properly recorded or delivered, permissions arbitrarily withheld or delayed, boorishly conducted searches or discourtesies of all kinds, petty harassments or unthinking neglect—many of them directly or indirectly affecting an inmate's movement or even release, which explains why the resultant outbursts often seem so out of proportion to the size of the complaint. A guard may accidentally forget to complete some small administrative chore that can cost the inmate a pass or even something more simple, like his weekly prison visit with his friends. When you have precious little to look forward to in any case, that weekly visit becomes a fairly important event in your life, and while the guard might quite rightly point out that all this noise over a two-hour visit seems a trifle excessive, he's missing the sense of scale necessary to understand an inmate's world. The inmate, from his point of view, is of course quite inclined to see the omission as an example of malicious negligence; the guard may see it as a trival oversight. Both are in effect right, which connotes the worst kind of dispute to arbitrate inasmuch as neither party feels in the least called upon to change his mind.

Another major area of guard-inmate conflict (I use the term "guard" loosely as inmates do, i.e., to include all general bureaucratic or security personnel) involves the business of official versus unofficial truth. One hard and fast rule you learn the day you enter prison is not to believe anything you hear and only half of what you see, and if an official said it, make that double. Unfortunately I must confirm that I found the rule generally applicable, and can't in fact think of any other organization where I've been fed so many lies, half-truths or misrepresentations. Much of the deception is perpetrated to "keep the peace," to avoid outbreaks of anger or even riot in the face of new rulings, policies or Parole or Review Board decisions. (It reminded me of a similar policy

I've never been able to tolerate or accept in the medical world, where many doctors persist in keeping patients and their families in the dark about the true state of the patient's health on the assumption that this will minimize everyone's anxiety. In fact, it does nothing of the sort, but rather breeds suspicion and distrust.)

Many Corrections officers actually control their charges by this method, promising inmates under their authority all sorts of baubles, weekend leaves, early parole considerations, special passes and the like, provided they work hard and jump when they're told. I was always amazed at how gullible inmates could be under those circumstances, anxiously scurrying to every beck and call, trying to keep up their "credit rating" in the right places.

Finally, when the big disappointment comes (as it invariably does), the blame somehow always lands on the higher-ups, the spin of the wheel or the roll of the dice. Actually, every guard knows (and I have one particular officer in mind who was single-handedly responsible for so much mental anguish among inmates in this connection that I sometimes wondered how he slept at night) that he has virtually no control over such decisions and that he is at most able to write a supporting memo, which is rarely worth more than the paper it's written on. The upshot of such methods, however, is that the suddenly enlightened inmate promptly becomes an inveterate guard/official hater, or at very least a sullen and uncooperative prisoner now beyond the reach of any subsequent appeal for participation in rehabilitative programs or such. And in the meantime, more evidence has been found to corroborate the profile of the treacherous malicious guard, and the wheel goes round again.

I should point out, however, that the quality of guards differs markedly from prison to prison, and that this difference is often directly related to the quality of the prison itself. When new guards were transferred to Stave Lake Camp, for example, they had to be considerably "retrained" to fit into the somewhat less volatile prison camp scene. Compared with the guards already stationed there, they tended for the first week or so to appear like little army commanders, barking orders and throwing tantrums and being so paranoid, they sometimes had to be quite firmly taken in hand by guards longer in residence. My general impression of Haney Correctional guards while I was in that Centre parallels this description; they were for the most part overbearing, peevish, tired and fed up, while those at SLC were a much more relaxed lot, older and more experienced.

There was, for example, old Ike McLaughlin, the Stave Lake road boss, a logger and great storyteller who dated from the days of steam-and-armstrong and who was chiefly responsible for the road-building and boom operations around the camp. He was a quick-tempered man who disliked foul-ups with a passion, but he had a great sense of humor and a well-earned reputation for fairness and good will; it was not his style to stab anyone in the back. Art Kingdon, the retired army communications expert who busted me for the home brew described in Fragment 39, was a similarly trustworthy man, fair and genuinely concerned to help a prisoner along. He was less than patient with slackers and had the sharp authoritative bark of a sergeant with the troops, but he never hounded anyone and no one ever had cause to bring complaint against him while I was at Stave Lake. Bill Bullock, former master diver with the British Navy, was also a great storyteller and a lover of fishing and beer, preferably all at the same time on some hidden lake up country. He was consistently reasonable and even-handed and refused to be party to mindless harassment of any sort.

And there was Maurice Leverrier, the officer who ran Pine Ridge Camp, who was a slightly more controversial figure with a sharp tongue and an equally sharp manner, who stood for no nonsense and tended to make sure he got none. But him, too, I found in the final analysis equitable and forthright, a man who ran a tough and tight show under extremely difficult circumstances—Pine Ridge Camp wasn't exactly blessed with the highest caliber of inmates or guards—but who could be counted on to go to bat for an inmate if he felt the effort was worth it, and who wasn't afraid to stick his neck out with his superiors now and then to do so.

But the most remarkable man among the prison guards in the B.C. system, according to both long- and short-timers alike, was undoubtedly Principal Corrections Officer C. D. Walton, known to hundreds, perhaps thousands, of present and former inmates of B.C. prisons simply as "Kelly." Heavyset, beer-bellied, good-natured Kelly, who wore his uniform cap at a rakish angle and camouflaged a shrewd sagacity behind a Santa Claus exterior, combining it all with a degree of easy-going common sense that was as welcome as it was unexpected in the prison system.

He seemed, in fact, cast out of about as perfect a mold for that job as one could imagine, and I was only one of many who felt that way about the man. In an environment that ranks among the most caustic in the social landscape, in an atmosphere so corrosive it often breaks down not only its intended victims but their keepers as well, Kelly lounged unperturbedly through the turmoil, tossing off a few jokes here, calming a few ruffled cockfeathers there, gaining and retaining the respect of one of the roughest, most critical and least even-handed audiences ever faced by any man.

And it wasn't that he was an easy touch; you couldn't often put anything over on Kelly—after twenty-five years in the business the man knew every trick in the bag and then some—it was rather his ability to appreciate that everyday living rarely paralleled the rigid systems outlined in the Prison Book of Rules ("No you can't go take a piss. It says here on my sheet that toilets are open only from eight-thirty to nine. If you weren't released from Classification until ten that's not my problem; my procedures sheet says eight-thirty to nine. You'll have to wait till tomorrow."). The glorious thing about Kelly was that if you really needed to take a piss, Kelly would come up with the key.

After twenty-five years, in short, the man still hadn't become institutionalized; after a life of inhaling paranoia day in and day out, he still hadn't lost his natural sense of proportion.

Just how many ulcers he was hiding under his belt he never said and never showed; to all appearances he was indefatigably cheerful and unfazed by the surrounding combat. In the six months I knew him I never once saw him lose his temper or his humor; when fights broke out, when red tape drove someone crazy or when some crisis or other upheaved the camp, it was generally Kelly who eased the tension with a wisecrack remark or an easy grin. "Hell, guys, look at the bright side," he'd offer genially, handing around comradely claps on the back or a friendly punch to the shoulder. "You're only doing a couple of years; me, I'm doing life."

And so he was in a way; in retrospect I've thought that he might have been only half-joking, subconsciously or not. Twenty-five years of eight-hour days in jail is a lot of time, and it couldn't all have been easy. I know, for example, that Kelly spent a number of years guarding the criminally insane, which is about the toughest job a man in that business can hold. I've met a few of that kind myself, both Inside and Out, and I can verify the point. Such people can be about the most dangerous human beings you'll ever meet. What makes them so is not so much their peculiar ferocity, but the fact that they never seem to give you any advance notice before they attack. Normal people get angry, they become noisy, belligerent, they flash all sort of signals to warn you of their intentions. The criminally insane are often disarming, even charming, casual, busy with something totally unconnected with you, apparently preoccupied, and they'll stay that way

159

for days, weeks, even years, then suddenly without warning kill you.

"Hell, all you had to do was show them the front of your back for half a second sometimes," Kelly once described it to me, chortling; "and they'd be onto you in a flash, trying to put a shiv through your gut." And he laughed some more, not in the least offended. "I guess if somebody wants to take my life I suppose I can't keep him from trying," I remember him saying in that connection on another occasion, "but I guess I can sure try to foul up his plans."

He must have had a few scuffles with inmates in his time (I never met a guard who hadn't), but he rarely mentioned any. The incidents in which he was known to have been involved were more along the lines of the one in which two young escapees, who had just cleared the perimeter fence, met Kelly as they were charging toward the parking lot. "You try to stop us and we'll slash you good!" they yelled, swinging two ugly-looking machetes they'd managed to get their hands on somewhere, possibly the machine shop. "Wouldn't dream of it," Kelly is reported to have assured them affably as he stepped aside to let them gallop past. "And have a nice trip."

To the most common, often unthinking threat one hears around prisons ("You wait'll I get out, man; I'll get your ass the day I walk out those gates!") Kelly had a stock reply. "Oh well, you might be able to land a few on me before my daughter gets to you," he'd drawl pleasantly, "but I've got to warn you about her; she's all of three and she's a holy terror!"

I think what I valued above all else in this man was the certainty that he could be totally trusted, not only by his allies but by everyone. "Talking to the guards" was a dangerous habit in Haney and even in some of its satellite prison camps, but talking to Kelly didn't qualify as part of the same category. I once overhead him in the Administration Office at Stave Lake Camp, talking to a very upset inmate who had just been denied some application or other. "Hey now, you know how the game in this place works, Jack," he admonished the man comfortably, no doubt pushing up his cap and re-settling it over his head in a characteristic gesture. "You can't go around here blowing your fuses and expect to be left alone; they'll throw you back in the cells quicker'n you can blow a whistle or your nose. If you want to yell at anybody, yell at me, I don't mind. Go ahead, heave all the shit at me you want, jump up and down on my hat, put a grenade in your head and pull the pin. Doesn't bother me, and when you've finished you can get your ass back to work and still get out of here on time . . ."

There was more, but the squawk of the Citizen Band radio drowned it out and I had the pants I needed from the adjoining laundry room anyhow. I walked back to my hut thinking that somebody ought to do something nice for that guy sometime; just to hear that kind of language, to see that kind of attitude drifting around a prison was really something to hold on to.

And I saw it again the day he brought in two very young escapees from another prison camp to our north; they had spent several days lost in the bush and had finally stumbled onto the logging road leading to our camp, not realizing they were literally on their way back to jail. When Kelly's truck showed up around the corner, they dived into the bush, but he saw them and stopped the vehicle. He didn't go in after them, just called out that he knew they were there, and that if they felt like throwing in the towel at this point, here was a good opportunity. They were, in fact, about ready to quit, since they didn't know anything about staying alive in that rugged country they hadn't tried already, so they came out. I was in camp when they came in, cold, wet and famished. Kelly patted each one's shoulder companionably.

"Well, fellas," he said, "you do look like you've put in a pretty good couple of days' work out there. How about I buy you both a cup of good hot coffee?" Saying which, he herded them off to the cook shack for a bite.

161

I thought I was going to die. I woke up one morning just before Wake-Up and found the room spinning wildly, my gut lurching and heaving; I clawed my way to the window for some fresh air but outside the world was spinning too. I dropped my head between my legs and gulped the air as deeply as I could and that stopped it somewhat, but that was the only arrangement that did; raising my head even slightly started everything whirling again. I was stuck in that awkward position, unable to move.

Then my throat started to constrict and my legs went numb. I couldn't get air. It was thoroughly frightening; I felt as if I was choking to death. The harder I tried to breathe, the less air I seemed able to inhale. I kept seeing bright red and green dots before my eyes and had a terrific urge to vomit, although I hadn't eaten anything for almost twelve hours. The illness had come totally without warning and seemed entirely without demonstrable cause, and it had me in something of a panic. I wore an oxygen mask all the way into Mission, where the ambulance delivered me to the district hospital.

I was kept there for only four or five hours while they ran a number of tests, then transferred to Haney's own hospital. Everything calmed down in due course, and by the third day I was no longer overly uncomfortable, although still periodically nauseous. I don't think they ever decided what it was, or if they did, they didn't tell me.

So I was in Haney again, a place I'd hoped never to set foot in again, and it was an odd perspective, seeing the prison through its hospital. The experience was a little like following the progress of a war from the inside of a Red Cross unit stationed just behind the front lines: each fracas or uproar spilled its casualties into either the hospital or the Hole, which was just down the corridor to our left. Most of those injured received only brief first-aid treatment and disappeared, but those who stayed were a curious lot. Mostly, I think, they were psychiatric rather than physical patients.

One tall, rather lanky fellow with big buck teeth and prematurely balding scalp (he was about twenty-five) sat sullenly in a corner all day long, rarely talking to anyone and on those few occasions when he did, bruskly demanded to know the time. There was a large clock in plain view above the unit door, a fact that was pointed out to him on virtually each occasion, but he paid no attention. I watched him closely for a while and decided that he wasn't necessarily being sullen at all, but rather that his face had simply settled into a sullen expression which he never bothered to change. His eyes changed all the time, however. He flatly refused to talk to me and seemed even afraid of me for some reason.

Another, younger inmate, half Indian I think, walked around the unit all day trailing his fingers over anything he could reach. Bedspreads, radiators, windowsills, doorknobs and furniture; he touched everything. It used to drive the two fellows from Boulder Bay Camp half mad because they played chess fairly often and Shakey (as he was called) would drift by, trailing his fingers over their heads and down over the chess figures (knocking most of them down) and onward, humming a little tune that was really more like the buzzing of a small electric motor. It was strictly forbidden to man-handle Shakey since he was obviously slightly flipped and presumably not intentionally a pain in the ass, so as soon as Shakey approached, the two would leap up and steer him clear of the board, aiming him in another direction. Per-sonally, I wasn't at all sure that the little bugger didn't know exactly what he was doing, and that he simply delighted in getting away with murder.

The two fellows from Boulder Bay were legitimate physical patients all right; they'd fallen into a patch of some poisonous plant and had broken out in extravagant rashes. They hadn't wanted to come to hospital at all and were fiercely anxious to get back to their camp; it was one of those Outward Bound programs which specializes in revving up the competitive in-stincts of young "insufficiently motivated" inmates, on the principle that once this instinct is sufficiently aroused, the competitive spirit will carry the youngsters back into Outside life and help them develop the pattern of success that today's society requires. To this end the instructors give and take points for absolutely everything, from personal deportment (language, dress, bearing, degree of enthusiasm expressed, rapport with instructors, inmates, etc.) to bushland survival techniques.

The two came in totally glassy-eyed, still feverishly "in the program" and thoroughly dismayed at their bad luck; points were being deducted for being sick, and each day was costing them five. I don't think the two were ever really in the hos-pital during their entire stay; they didn't pay the slightest attention to their surroundings, but sat across from each other on their beds jabbering furiously away about "the program," keeping each other at a fever pitch, or busily per-forming exercises on an "exercise court" they'd created by pushing two beds as far apart as possible and laying blankets on the tiled floor as mats. I had to admit they were in excellent shape physically and they played a mean game of chess, but I did find their "enthusiasm expressed" a bit forbidding.

We had another fellow in for a short while who kept bursting into tears and letting himself fall full weight against the metal door jambs, on several occasions opening nasty-looking cuts on his head and face. He was finally released because his time was up, but had he committed a more serious offense (he was in on a charge of possession of stolen property) with a longer sentence, I'd hate to think what might have happened to him. The consensus was that he was "faking it" and I'm not saying he wasn't, in a weird sort of way, but the consistency of his behavior sometimes made me wonder if there wasn't more to it than met the eye.

We had an Indian inmate, who didn't actually live in the unit but came in each day as a day patient, who was the fattest human being I've ever personally met or seen. He had something wrong with his foot and would sit in the T.V. room all day with his foot in some chemical bath, watching the day's television programs. I stayed away from him because he pawed at people all the time and I hate being pawed at. He was still sitting there with his foot bath when I finally left.

I often wondered why some of these men were even in jail, but I only found out in the faker's case. I tried on one occasion to ask Shakey and he looked at me in a deeply thoughtful way for some moments, then drifted away without answering. When I called him back and asked the question again, he looked very thoughtful a second time, then glanced at me uncertainly and said, "Swipin cars?" in a hopeful voice. He was either a superb con man or he simply couldn't remember anymore.

As far as I could tell, the "hospital" was in effect only a holding unit in disguise; none of the patients there were receiving any treatment other than pills, and these were prescribed by two part-time doctors whom I never actually saw.

There were no special facilities for anything, not even special diets, so for the first three days while my stomach was settling down, I ate nothing at all. Once every few days someone asked me if I was feeling better; otherwise nothing of a medical nature was undertaken. That suited me well enough at the time; I read a lot of books and watched a little T.V. and slept a lot. Even so, I didn't get out of the place nearly as soon as I wanted; like the rest of prison, it was only effortlessly entertaining for the first half a dozen days.

I remember the night before I was scheduled to leave the hospital quite clearly because they'd installed a new arc lamp in the prison parking lot below our windows without paying any attention to the fact that the hospital had no curtains. The bluish light lit up the unit with an eerie neon intensity, making sleep almost impossible. I was one of the last to fall asleep that night as far as I could tell, and it must have been about 3:00 A.M. when I did. Half an hour later I woke up with a start and looked around; most of the others were up as well, listening to Shakey. He appeared to be asleep, and was singing one of the most note-perfect renditions of Elvis's "Blue Suede Shoes" I've ever heard. He sang at the top of his voice, beautifully clear in melody and superbly in tune. We were all totally stunned and nobody did anything to interrupt. Shakey sang the whole song twice, then subsided back into silence. We all looked at each other questioningly for some moments, then wordlessly went back to sleep. Nobody mentioned the incident at all the next day.

I'm asleep in a bunk in Hut Six at Pine Ridge Camp. I've been sick for almost two weeks at Haney Correctional Centre's hospital and am being transferred back to Stave Lake via this place; a truck is to pick me up in the morning. I'm dreaming of great urgencies, pressing engagements; massive steamrollers lumber back and forth across my gut.

I awake with an agonizing effort as if my mind were embedded in sticky toffee, pull slightly free of my somnolent numbness and come upright in that mindless way a figurine with water in its base bobs erect when tipped over. No question about it, I have to take one helluva piss.

Now where is everything? This is Pine Ridge, they don't have toilets in the huts, you have to cut across the prison compound all the way to the other side, to the "Ablution Hut." (My mind registers a tiny concussion in my nostrils; by god, I've just snickered; guess I still can't get over that idiotic name.) But that's a whole expedition in itself; it's out of the question, the urgency is too great. I'll probably have cold sores in the morning anyway; isn't that what you get if your bladder is under pressure for too long? Bullshit, who told me that? I think it was Suzanne; yeah, was Suzanne. Hm.

I fumble around in the dark for my shorts and fumble them on. Foot through the hole there; synchronize, synchronize. Jesus. Nobody should have to be up this time of night, for any reason. I stop my breathing and listen. Nobody is.

Suzanne, yes indeed. Hm.

I rise precariously from the bunk and feel my way to the door.

Outside the moon is a bright blur through cloudy haze; I squint with much effort to bring it into focus but I've forgotten my glasses and I'm almost blind without them. Spotlight beams ricochet silently around the compound; all is vacant and eerie, like violence finally exhausted or paralyzed. I step gingerly off the stoop and onto the gravel; I've also forgotten to put on my shoes, goddamn it.

Now where, what? Out here on the driveway? Good lord no, that's indecent. Over there, that bush has the irresistible come-hither look. That's it, that's the one.

I tap painfully across the jagged gravel and thankfully onto the grass. Take up stance before bush. A bird in the hand. There she parabolas. Sweet Jesus Murphy, blessed relief. I'm about to melt into a puddle of pure bliss, when *wham!* I'm hit without warning by a brilliant blast of light, which bursts over me like an anti-aircraft searchlight beam, turning my arc of urine into a steady stream of shattered glass.

"Hey you! What the hell you doing!"

A guard pounds across the gravel toward me, breaking into the shaft of light, a grotesque silhouette.

"Stop that, you hear me! You stop that right bloody now!"

He must be kidding, surely. I mean, I'm already what you might call totally committed, my friend; the dynamite is lit. You're trying to order a suicide not to jump when he's already over the side and halfway down. Besides, even if I did what you might call nip myself in the bud, just what do you expect me to do with it?

I keep pissing steadily, unwavering.

The guard slows to a stop beside me, out of breath and, suddenly, out of words. What do you do or say to a bleary-eyed half-asleep fellow human innocently engaged in the act of righteous self-voidance at god knows what hour of the morning? You certainly don't grab at him any more than you'd grab at a turned-on fire hose, and for similar reasons.

So we just stand there in the blazing spotlight, companionably, helpless. There's really nothing to do but wait.

"You know that's against regulations," he finally ventures, mostly to fill in time while pretending not to watch the sparkling flow.

"Oh, I wouldn't be at all surprised," I nod agreeably, wondering how my capacity is holding out. It's a bit like smoking your last cigar before a firing squad; the longer it lasts, the longer you live.

I piss on, hopefully.

The guard, being totally unable to do anything about his dutiful outrage, begins to lose it; I can practically feel it ebbing out of him. I feel sorry about that and try to make him more comfortable.

"Hell of a time to have to be working, eh?"

He shrugs, uncertain, slightly upset at having no other options than to be friendly. But he's a sociable sort for all that, trained to say please and thank you. "Well, it's not all that bad. Cooler this time of night."

He swivels his neck to stare dubiously at the moon above the flag pole. I turn slightly to follow his gaze and he steps back abruptly. "Oh sorry," I offer hastily, scrambling to correct my aim. "I'm so damn blind without my glasses. Couldn't see the broad side of a barn door if I had me a dozen of these eyes. Didn't get your boot, did I?"

It appears I haven't. Just as well no doubt.

The beat goes on.

The guard begins to be curious. "What the hell you been drinkin, for chrissake? You must have pissed a quart already —you got diarrhea or something?"

"Yeah, I'm a bit surprised myself. Must have been that tea I had at brew-up; drank off four cups last night. Also just did a little time in sick bay up at Haney; that might have something to do with it. My gut still doesn't seem entirely back in business."

"Sick bay, no shit." The guard is relieved; now there's something to talk about. We've been standing here under the moon far too long to go back to the robot-victim routine; he's been troubled about how to handle this after I reassemble myself back into my shorts, I can see that clearly. And the stream is definitely tapering off; he can see that clearly too. Only a few more seconds of reserves left to go.

And that takes care of that. A good flick for good measure and I haul in all lines. Everything secured and hatches battened down. The time has come, the walrus said.

I turn and look at him expectantly, directly into his face, waiting. And suddenly, without warning, the advertising jingle pops into my head, and before I have time to think about it or stop myself I hear myself asking him very politely:

"Will that be cash, or Chargex?"

*　　　*　　　*

About half a year later after I got out of prison I met that same guard in the Legion beer parlor in Mission, B.C. We bought each other a few drinks and told the story to the others sitting around the table and all of us had a good laugh over it. He kept spluttering: "An' you shoulda seen this squirt, standin there like a moon calf half blind an' lookin around with those dazed-lookin eyes, an' then he sticks his whanger

170

back in his pants an' turns to me like a goddamn bank clerk an' says: 'Will that be cash, or Chargex?' " And we all crack up again; he's a good storyteller, but I feel compelled to remind him: "Yeah, but you still put me on charge anyway, you chintzy bugger," which doesn't faze him at all because, as he righteously points out to me and the others around the table: "I mean, you were pissin on the Queen's lawn, after all; you can't get away with pissin on the Queen's lawn."

43

When I woke up the next morning it was already 6:30 A.M. and nobody had come to wake me up to catch the truck back to Stave. I dressed hurriedly and hastened over to the office to find out what was going on.

"Say, didn't the Stave Lake truck come through this morning?"

The guard gazed at me carefully with an owlish look.

"Yup; went through here at six."

"Well, why wasn't I called? I was supposed to be on that truck."

The guard turned slightly in the squeaky office chair and settled his feet on the desk. He looked displeased.

"Tell you what. You just leave it up to us to decide what you should and what you shouldn't be on. We know what the fuck we're doing. Got that?"

If I'd been half as confident as he was that they knew what they were doing, I wouldn't have been in the office asking to know what was going on. "Well, what am I being held here for then? How come you let me miss that truck?"

The guard swung his legs off the desk and got up abruptly. He was even more displeased.

"You didn't *miss* that truck, goddammit; you weren't supposed to be on it! Now get your butt outta here before I heave you out!"

I closed the door behind me and stood on the porch, angry and mystified and worried. What the hell were they keeping me here for? Just what was going on *this* time? I didn't trust this Pine Ridge bunch overly much; they were famous for "holding back" transient inmates if their work crews were incomplete and I had no intention of getting side-tracked into this dump. They could and did get away with it though. The general level of efficiency and communication was so poor, and the degree to which nobody really gave a damn so considerable, they could easily "forget" or "mislay" an inmate's papers for weeks or months while they made use of his specific expertise (particularly if he was a mechanic, carpenter or truck driver) to their heart's content. Unfortunately for me in this case, I had been trained at Stave Lake to repair and rebuild chain saws, and they knew about that. By the time I'd finished breakfast and was standing for Morning Count (still nobody had told me what was going on) I was positive that that's what they had in mind: they wanted me to fix their fleet of chain saws. The cook had told me that they didn't have a mechanic here and that the saws were falling apart.

The count took a long time and then the guards changed over, the day shift taking over from the night staff, and when that was finally accomplished they began to hand out the work detail. Inmate after inmate was called and directed to some job or crew, until finally I was the only one left still standing on the wide driveway, waiting. The trucks drove off and the crews trotted away and then the Officer of the Day motioned me into the office. I entered and stood against the counter, not saying anything.

173

He looked me over briefly. "Those the best clothes you got?"

"That's right. All my other clothes are at Stave."

"Hm," he grunted. And then: "You're going for your parole interview."

My mind stopped short, then reeled and recoiled like a kicked slot machine. So that was it! And then the full impact of what he had just said hit me and I virtually exploded across the counter.

"But that's impossible! I haven't got anything here! Hell, I've been spending weeks and months preparing my documentation; I've got a whole shoebox of supporting letters up at Stave; I've got a formal job offer and all sorts of official affadavits sitting at that camp; this is ridiculous; you're telling me to go to a parole interview with no supporting material at all!"

The officer shrugged and let it pass. "All I know is that they want to see you at ten o'clock," he said, pointing out my name on the day's Movement Sheet (A. P. SCHROEDER, 7748651 PRC to HCC: Parole Interview 10:00 A.M.) and handing me a blue gate pass. "Show this paper to the guy at the Main Gate."

I took the pass in a daze, still not fully believing this mess. For months I'd been preparing for this interview, waiting for it, imagining it; ever since I'd been booked into Oakalla I'd been busily writing and soliciting letters of support, organizing future plans, filling out applications, filling in forms, discussing strategy with my counselors and waiting impatiently for my eligibility date to arrive to set the whole machinery in motion. Now without warning it had begun, and I was sitting empty-handed in a side-track holding camp, dressed in torn and ill-fitting khaki, unkempt and unprepared and, for the moment at least, thoroughly frantic. What a rotten piece of luck! To endanger an almost certain chance at parole just because of a hitch in timing. I'd expected all sorts of possible

174

twists, but not this one. What a bitch! I turned to the officer and pointed to the phone.

"Any chance you could get me a postponement on this thing?"

He shrugged and gave a short, harsh laugh. "You sure you want to wait another two months before they get around to you again?"

I could see his point. "No, I guess you're right. I guess I'll just see what I can accomplish with this one."

I scuffed off to the washrooms to try to make myself look as presentable as I could.

*   *   *

Back at the Centre, the secretary told me to sit down on a wooden bench in the corridor and wait. "She's still busy," she told me firmly, as if expecting an argument about it. "She'll call you when it's time."

I sat down on the crude bench outside the office and stared at the ashtray beside the door; it was made from an old automobile wheel someone had welded onto a stand. Then I stared at the ugly green corridor and then I stared at my shoes, which were about ready for the trashcan. Damn; what a crummy break. Faced with this unexpected piece of bad luck, alarmed that my application wouldn't be considered under the most ideal circumstances, I suddenly found myself having to face just how badly I really wanted to get out of here, how desperately I'd been counting on getting out by the end of the first year at least, and how I'd in fact been living on an emotional budget geared to that schedule.

Of course I'd demurred whenever anyone had suggested I'd be paroled at first crack (one of the first survival tactics an inmate learns: always expect the worst), but now I realized with considerable unease that I hadn't sufficiently *believed* my own demurral, that underneath it I had secretly decided I probably *would* get out the first time around, and that I hadn't really prepared myself for a possible refusal at all.

That was unwise. In fact, that was dangerous; to live without considerable safety margins in prison was to risk the very method by which one tended to survive. It was living intellectually beyond one's emotional means—a gamble that was rarely worth the risks. Damn it again. I flexed my fingers and cracked my knuckles and finally got up to walk it off; up and down the corridor past the office door, watching the tiles sliding away under my feet, square after square, square after square, square after square . . .

"Miss Stearman will see you now."

Miss Stearman was a brisk and efficient-looking young woman, pleasant in a cold sort of way and very official. She fixed me with a searching stare.

"So you're the young man who's been causing all this uproar."

I didn't know what she was talking about. I must have looked perplexed.

"Well, I'd like to tell you right away, Mr. Schroeder, before we proceed any further, that I for one will not be snowed by your avalanche of letters, and that if my investigations result in the slightest doubt as to the acceptability of your proposed future plans, we are quite prepared to let you stew in here for your full term."

"To let me what?"

Miss Stearman realized she'd gone too far and back-pedaled slightly. "I mean we're under no obligation whatsoever to grant you a parole; parole is a discretionary privilege, not a right, and if we have any doubts at all about your eligibility we are quite prepared not to grant your application."

I was still puzzled at the course this interview was taking. I couldn't figure out what I might have done to provoke such a frontal attack.

"Miss Stearman, could you just clarify for me what you

meant by 'refusing to be snowed' by my letters? Could we, in fact, start all over again from the beginning? I'm not sure I understand this outburst at all. What exactly have I done, as it appears I have, to offend you?"

Miss Stearman sat down at her desk and stared at a point just above my head. She didn't seem in the least disconcerted.

"What I'm saying, Mr. Schroeder, is that I refuse to be impressed by a lot of friends trying to overwhelm the Parole Board offices with mail, and that I will not let them side-track me from a thorough investigation of this case."

This was becoming ridiculous. What the hell did this woman want? to interview me or just to fire pistols into the air?

"Miss Stearman, when I entered prison almost six months ago I didn't know the first thing about the rules and regulations here. All I knew was that I wanted to get out of here as soon as possible, and I made many inquiries as to the best way to achieve that goal. What I was told by my counselors was to 'secure community support,' as much as possible. I asked whether they really meant 'as much as possible'; did they mean even fifty or a hundred supporting letters if I could get them? The answer was an emphatic yes.

"So I went to work soliciting support from people I knew, as you have seen. I didn't blackmail people for it and I didn't twist their arms; I solicited their help on the assumption that I was doing myself a favor, that I was stockpiling credits toward an early release. I would not have done so had I realized it would result in so much difficulty. I want to get out of here as badly as the next man and am not particularly interested in putting myself in a bad light. I'm not asking for special favors, and my documentation is entirely at your disposal. But I don't want to begin with any disadvantages either, and your suggestion that my supporting letters campaign is in some way dishonest implies this. I wish to protest against such an implication."

Miss Stearman looked annoyed. "Are you aware, Mr.

177

Schroeder, of how many letters most inmates submit to support their application?"

"No, I'm not."

"Well, I'll tell you. About four, Mr. Schroeder, maybe at the most five or six."

"In view of what I've just explained to you, I don't see the point."

Miss Stearman refused to be side-tracked. "And do you know at this point how many letters accompanied *your* application?"

"Not exactly. I sent out a lot of requests."

"Eighty-four letters, Mr. Schroeder. Exactly eighty-four to date, although I gather they're still dribbling in. Tell me, are you by any chance related to the entire staff of the Canadian Broadcasting Corporation?"

I flashed her a lopsided grin. "No, I'm just naturally enthusiastic."

"That's what I mean, Mr. Schroeder; *that's* the sort of thing I'm talking about. Maybe you're just a little too enthusiastic for your own good. A little too self-confident perhaps. Maybe you haven't learned your lesson from all this yet. Maybe we should just wait until you do."

The lady was getting to be a bit much. "Do you by any chance have any *personal* interest in this case, Miss Stearman?" I found myself asking as evenly as I could, a flush of anger tightening through my chest and neck. "Are you on some sort of personal vendetta? On some private crusade?"

Miss Stearman ignored that icily and took another tack. "The prison report informs me you've been ill," she noted, flipping through several pages on her desk. "Do you often become ill before important interviews?"

"I'm afraid I don't follow you."

"I'm merely pointing out that your illness came at a very convenient point in time, wouldn't you say? You just happen to get ill a week before your parole interview, before your application is to be investigated. Did the prospect of this

178

meeting really cause such a furor in your system that you had to spend over a week in this institution's hospital just preceding it? Did you think you could extract a little extra sympathy that way?"

I'll admit I almost slugged her. She came within a hair's-breadth of getting it right between the eyes for that one, and I think she sensed it too because during her subsequent interviews with my family and my "future employer" (just for the duration of the parole) she kept mentioning my "hostility," how I was trying to con the Parole Board, and so on. When I returned to Stave Lake the next day I immediately began making inquiries about her, trying to find out just who she was and if she had any credibility whatsoever. The camp officers had never seen her before and were of the opinion that either she was just an overly paranoid beginner who had run into a bit more than she could handle, or (more likely) she'd been intentionally trying to provoke me to flush out any "additional information" in which the Parole Board might have been interested.

I didn't care to speculate about the provocation, but if her purpose had been to lob a grenade or two into my life just for the hell of it, she'd managed that with admirable skill. The prospect of having my application handled by that particular female contributed considerably to sleepless nights and scheming days, devising and rejecting plan after plan to counteract what I imagined her strategy might be. I almost reached the point of dropping the whole idea of parole completely, inasmuch as I discovered that parole isn't simply a free pass out of jail anyway; there are considerable risks involved. For one thing, a Parole Board can withdraw your parole at a moment's notice and for any reason; there is no court procedure to cover such decisions, and no appeal; a parole officer can yank you off the street for something as vague as "poor attitude" if he likes, and there is nothing you can do about it.

Furthermore, if you "violate parole" in any way and are

pulled back Inside, all the time you have spent Outside while on that parole is lost to you; your sentence is calculated to resume from the day you left prison to begin that parole. It is therefore possible for a man to get paroled after one-third of his sentence, go out and spend all but *one day* on the street and then get yanked back on that last day to do a full two-thirds of his sentence all over again, and this time with little or no chance for another parole. That's a fairly weighty risk for an inmate to consider, particularly if his life style tends to drift him through a lot of pubs, bars or night clubs where the chances of committing a parole violation are extremely high. Even a minor pub dispute is enough to do it.

Many paroles also restrict an inmate to certain geographic or municipal areas, and some even refuse him the consumption of alcohol or hold him to an early-evening curfew. I saw some that directed that the parolee not come into contact with certain named persons, or specified that he stay out of certain parts of certain towns. Most "experienced" inmates won't even accept a parole of that sort since they know perfectly well they would violate those regulations five times a day, and the risk simply isn't worth it.

In my case, admittedly, those risks weren't a major concern and so I eventually came to my senses and rejected the idea of cancelling the application. I began instead to work on bringing my expectations down from their previous dangerously high level. Within a couple of weeks I'd convinced myself that there was a good chance I'd have to do about another year anyway, and once that idea became firmly established I found myself relaxing considerably about the whole parole business, even to the point of beginning to live with the idea of spending Christmas in jail.

My cell mates knew what I was doing and helped me along, pointing out the fickleness of Parole Board decisions, the acreage of red tape involved in all applications, the ill-fated interview and the increasing stiffness of Parole Board guidelines. The public was getting very unhappy about the idea of parole, they reminded me; the likelihood of getting paroled at first crack, for long-timers and even for first offenders like me, was obviously decreasing. Besides, Christmas in jail wasn't all that bad; they usually trotted out some performance or other and everybody got a care package of canteen-type stuff from some local do-gooders, and lots of ice cream. And you didn't even have to work on Boxing Day.

So I settled back into the routine again, fixing chain saws and writing production reports and trying to make my cell look like home.

FRAGMENT

44

Ten o'clock in the morning. The crews have been in the bush since seven o'clock; only one guard is left in camp and he's out of sight somewhere. I'm supposed to be converting raw production statistics into a formal progress report in the storeroom, but I feel restless. The apparent peacefulness makes me jumpy, like an animal in a forest suddenly too still.

I begin walking slowly through the buildings, feeling once again as if I've been here for years and years, a tired old child in a worn-out playpen; room after room reminds me of the inmates who have lived inside them, climbed these walls, thrown tantrums on these bunks, sat legs dangling over the side endlessly talking over plans plans plans, filling out form after form, worrying about Street affairs, wives, kids, lovers, enemies, helplessly raging at their own helplessness, the fucking red tape, the close-meshed net of rules entangling us all. Furious outbursts, swearing, sweating, fist-shaking—and in Room Three old Joe the cleaner, pushing his broom ahead of himself more slowly every day, muttering in Russian about bureaucrats and revolution. Calendars everywhere, the days x'ed out, numbers circled.

And then finally they are gone as if they've never been here; new ones throw their cardboard boxes or sacks into the corners and drop onto the bunks, still staring slowly at nothing in particular. You leave them alone for the first hour or so; that's understood. But you can tell almost immediately whether or not they'll make it; no special way to tell, you just know. You can practically smell it on them after a while. We used to lay bets within five minutes sometimes.

The first escape I witnessed involved a fellow who had flunked that test hands down; he was a misfit, a kid far out of his depth, and they hounded him with all the instinctive vindictiveness of an animal pack shedding its diseased or disabled members. When he finally fled, barefoot and coatless into the bush, his room looked as if a bomb had exploded inside; torn and scattered books, clothing, up-ended bed and mattress, all whirled throughout the room in indescribable chaos. An obscure note on the mattress babbled something about humankind and falseness, illusion and order; no one could make it out. He was caught several weeks after and re-turned to maximum security, where I saw him through the bars one day, listlessly nudging a mop along the corridor. His head was shaven, some teeth were missing and he had about him the unfocused look of a tranquilized dog. I called to him but he didn't look up.

FRAGMENT

45

When I looked at my calender this morning I discovered I have now been in prison half a year. It feels like an awfully long time. Somehow, Prison Time is Outside Time quadrupled or even more; in here you live by ontological rather than chronological time, the kind of time lived by drunks, by stoned or panicked people. Time Inside stretches irrationally in all directions, and most of all in length. And half a year Inside brings you to a point with respect to prisons as the age of thirty is supposed to bring you with respect to life.

By that I mean that after half a year, the surprises are over. You've tried most of the angles, or at least all the ones you want to try, and you've settled on the ones you want. You've developed a more or less successful formula to get you through, and if it isn't entirely successful, well, you're pretty well stuck with it anyway. At half a year in prison, the repetitions begin to occur so regularly that that's normally the point at which a long-timer draws in his horns, lets himself go numb and settles in for the ride, developing a steady, almost drugged rhythm that most effectively kills the time. If I had very much more time to do, I'd probably fall into that pattern too. Even prison can't keep a man intrigued forever.

It *was* intriguing, even fascinating, for a while, however, and while it was, it was like all very full experiences: simultaneously absorbing, frustrating, anxious, mysterious, ecstatic, boring. I came in through the front door in full regalia, armed to the teeth with convictions, assumptions, certainties and confidence; all the ragtag clutter of wisdom I thought I'd discovered or made my own; I feel considerably lightened of much of that now. Much of it, it seems, hasn't managed to survive the massive assault of prison reality.

I discovered, for example, that I didn't really know "most people" at all, though in my conversation I used that phrase all the time—"most people do this, most people do that"—in fact, I think there probably isn't any such thing; "most people" are simply those people whom we don't personally know and therefore don't understand. It seems curious that with only very few exceptions, each inmate I came to know to any extent eventually made sense to me, so that in each case his crimes weren't simply an evil thing he'd committed, but an understandable one. Which doesn't mean I'm suggesting we let everyone go free just because their crimes are understandable, but it does seem to imply that people who don't make sense to us are probably simply people we haven't gotten to know, and so our disagreements with them are by the same token probably more often than not groundless. Whatever else this realization implied to me, it meant that it was probably a risky business to go around making assumptions about what most people think or feel, since the characteristics ascribed to "them" (i.e., others) generally never ended up applying to anyone I'd really gotten to know. They always applied to "the others" whom I hadn't, coincidentally, yet met.

There are other things. When I first entered prison I bitterly missed good music, the presence of women, the absence of noise, good books, good food. I wouldn't want to do without any of these any more now than I did then, but I've discovered that I can, and I have. Knowing this has given me a sense of self-sufficiency that I've grown to value highly; in prison you learn to travel light, with nothing in your sack but what you can afford to lose anyway (because you probably will) and everything you really need tucked safely in your head, out of sight. To live extravagantly in prison is dangerous; you have to spend all your time defending your excesses, and you can very easily go down with them. A balloon-size ego, of course, also falls into this category, and was for me, as for many, a major difficulty; of all places in the world, prisons are probably the major battleground for inflated or insecure egos.

That one, like most personal difficulties, seems finally to be rooted in the question of Identity, which Inside is a particularly pronounced problem. Since many men in prison have an exaggerated sense of who they are (which often camouflages an equally large uncertainty on that score), they also tend to have an exaggerated sense of what they need to live, which in an environment of so little space and so much pressure is an explosive mixture. Invariably, this makes a man unpredictable, quick to take offense and quick to give it; if one man calls another a fuckhead or a goof, and that man is unsure of his own identity, he has perforce to assume that that may indeed be a possible description of himself, and feel obliged to fight about it. When two men walk into a thousand-cubic-foot room, each totally convinced he needs seven hundred and fifty cubic feet of it, they again have little choice but to fight. It is therefore of inestimable value to know for certain that you *aren't* a fuckhead or a goof; the only response required is then a cheerful shrug and something like: "Sorry, I've checked that one out pretty carefully and that's definitely not me."

It was for me also particularly useful to discover that there need be no relationship at all between the size of one's self-esteem and the amount of space to accommodate it. If I ran into someone who was thoroughly convinced he needed all the room there was (a not unusual case Inside), it cost me nothing at all to simply let him have it; absence of space eventually made no inroads on my sense of self at all. That also meant I was able to get much closer to people in a very short time, since I simply stopped threatening them in the ways they'd become accustomed to being threatened.

That, as a matter of fact, led me to another realization I'd suspected beforehand and eventually confirmed for myself in jail: the fact that it's not at all necessary to have enemies. I used to think that having no enemies implied blandness of thought, a wishy-washy, all-purpose attitude in which everything was right as long as it pleased everyone, etc. It is, I think, a fairly common standby of the intellectual community. What I discovered instead was that enemies are rarely if ever made because of divergent opinions, and that people who hate each other do so because they feel they are being slighted, insulted or in some way undermined, not merely because they hold differing opinions on some subject or other.

I had many opportunities to test this for myself Inside, because inmates more than most are people who feel they've never been paid adequate or serious attention to, and who tend to be overly defensive about this. That's one big reason why they're constantly so ready to fight at the slightest provocation. I found that if I listened (I mean *really* listened) to them very carefully and showed that I'd understood what they'd been saying or trying to say (as opposed to necessarily agreeing with what they'd said) I had their instant friendship and could insist on any opinion I liked. That procedure, in fact, occurred quite naturally since I was extremely curious about how inmates thought and lived (thinking of them at that time as a somehow quite different species, I suppose).

Eventually I realized that they weren't anything special

at all, and that we were simply a carbon copy of anybody's telephone book or voters' list who happened to be living out part of our lives in a slightly unnatural environment. Because the only difference between the Inside and the Outside is that Inside the experiment we call civilization is conducted in a hothouse, pressure-cooker atmosphere, which naturally produces its results unusually quickly and often with unusual emphasis. Otherwise, the ingredients are the same: men struggling for power, fame, love; men hounded by excesses or deficiencies in themselves colliding with each other in the dark; men blinded by ignorance or eroded self-confidence continually stumbling into the high-speed traffic of those whose lives are always just disappearing over the next horizon. You see it every day on every street.

46

I was standing just outside the Tool Room a short distance from the propane tanks when Anderson, a former chemical plant junior executive in on a dope charge, shuffled by down the corridor dragging a broom. They'd kept him inside today where they could watch him; somebody had come in off a temporary pass yesterday and had told him about his wife. He'd already suspected something was wrong because she'd stopped answering his letters and hadn't come to see him in a month; but hearing it confirmed like that was another matter. He'd been prowling through the huts all morning, looking like ten sticks of taped dynamite with the fuse lit, and I could feel the violence coming off him like static-electric waves. He stopped beside the tanks in a preoccupied way, staring at nothing in particular and tapping his fist distractedly against the metal. That was where Alf the cook found him half an hour later when he came by to dump the garbage. "Cheer up, Anderson," he suggested, setting down his pails for a moment to flex his fingers. "Things aren't ever as bad as they seem."

That did it. Anderson blew like a lid off a burst pressure

cooker: "Aw, what the fuckin hell, it just makes no goddamn sense at all! What in bloody blazes that broad thinks she's doin I'm damned if I know! Just been bleedin me, bleedin me, bleedin me all her life; wants this, wants that, wants to fuck around the clock, but when I'm in a jam, when I'm cornered and need a little help, where d'you think the broad is then, eh? Where the hell is she then, by Christ!" He paced furiously up and down along the tanks. "So I can't keep up with all those goddamn fantasies, I mean a man's tired once in a while in his life; Jesus, like a bloody leech day and night and never gave a sweet damn about where it all came from! Shit, half the time I came in she wasn't even home! And now she gives me that 'oh god what have you done to us now' routine. Fuck, she was smokin that grass like a chimney while it was there, lots of times, and that never seemed to bother her then! The two-faced bitch! Aw, what can you do!"

He slammed his fist disgustedly against a tank, making it bong like an empty gas drum. "And then you end up in a hole like this, eatin fuckin cabbage and bein ordered around by a pack of dim-witted idiots who wouldn't know a whorehouse from an outhouse if their asses were stuck in one, half of 'em pill freaks and the other half alcoholics, surrounded by killers and macho freaks and god knows what else, while the dildo who runs this camp is still tryin to learn to chew bubble gum and hit his ass with both hands at the same time.

"Jesus Christ! Never should have come to this jerk-off province, it's just been one screw-up after another, brick on brick for god's sake; this goddamn place is jinxed, I tell you; there's somethin in the air that makes a man's spirit wilt and die, just fuckin roll over and die—every bloody time I come here it's the same! God almighty, man, I mean just what the hell is *happening* to my life?? Every bloody time I turn around it just keeps cavin in on me again and again; I mean it just doesn't make any sense! And now they hit me with a nine-month rap for a pound of grass! Christ, in Toronto they'd kiss

190

your ass for that and charge you two bits for the judge's bus fare! Goddamn cavemen in the courts around here probably still burn people at the stake for jaywalking! Nine months, for chrissake; nine months!

"And so you'd think maybe the little bitch might raise that dainty little ass of hers to stick her face into the visiting room now and then; maybe drop by the odd time to see her dear little monkey in his cage! But no, that'd be far too much trouble, wouldn't it; that might strain her little sternum getting up off her goddamn back! So instead she up and runs off with some goddamn hippy. A fuckin *hippy*, for god's sake! Can you even believe your ringin ears?! Takes the kids and packs her bags and follows some unwashed little pied piper into his macrobiotic sleeping bag, with not so much as a backward glance or a hat tip to your old yours truly! God! I suppose she's gonna raise those kids on karma and brown rice or some such bullshit. Thankless little shit!

"And I'm sittin here hog-tied like some animal in the slaughter yard where she no doubt hopes I'll rot and conveniently die! But I'll catch up with that little cunt. You bet your goddamn life I'll go after her and that little bastard if it takes me the rest of my life, and then I'll kill that little motherfucker, you hear me, I'll choke his mangy little throat! Thinks she'll let me burn out in this dung heap, but not this boy, mama; not this mother's only son! I'll get 'em both on the same lick, grab his long-haired ass and up-end him right into his own goddamn pot of soya beans or whatever the hell they eat; let him choke on that for a day or two.

"The little prick! Tear him apart like damned confetti, then rub her face in what's left! You can bet your goddamn life the minute I get out of this hole, just the very second they slam that gate behind me and I'm out, it's beeline tracks for the both of 'em; the bastard's days are numbered! If it's the very last thing I ever do! You just keep your eye on the fuckin obituaries!"

And suddenly seeing little Alf still sitting wide-eyed on his garbage pail, his mouth half-open in consternation: "And don't tell me things aren't ever as bad as they seem, you naïve little idiot!! They're fucked, kid, plain and simple; totally fucked!"

He stomped off toward Hut Two, exasperatedly slashing his broom at the weeds outside the steps. Alf continued to sit there on his pail, looking troubled. I stepped quietly back into my Tool Room and leaned against the bench, staring for a long time through the grimy window at whatever was beyond, thinking vaguely about toothpaste and how it never really seems to get your teeth quite white . . .

FRAGMENT

Without warning, I'm at Pine Ridge again. Late yesterday evening a guard suddenly stopped me on my way to the laundry room and told me to pack my stuff. "You're leaving on the morning truck," he said. I was so astonished I just stood there for a moment speechless while he walked away. When I chased after him to find out what was going on, he spread his hands and kept walking. "Could be almost anything," he shrugged, hitching up his belt and readjusting the aerial on his walkie-talkie. "All I know's you're going to Pine Ridge. Did you apply for anything there or at Haney?"

I took the question to be rhetorical; there wasn't a man at Stave Lake who hadn't applied for virtually everything on the menu: parole, work release, temporary absence, weekend leave, appeals on any of a dozen different decisions, educational releases. "It wouldn't be my parole, would it!" I suggested, starting with the most unlikely choice. "They'd have told you if it was my parole, wouldn't they?"

He agreed. "Maybe work release," he said. "I've heard of

a few of them getting through. Did you apply for a work release out of Pine Ridge Camp?"

"Yes, of course."

"Well, could be that's it. Maybe."

He didn't know or he wasn't saying. I lugged my sheets to the laundry room and returned to my hut to pack my possessions once again.

The leave-taking from Stave Lake was brisk and brief; friendships and enmities, arrivals and departures Inside are so unpredictable that inmates soon learn to live with the unexpected, and to keep the bonds of friendship only loosely tied. As various cell mates and fellow inmates came to say goodbye, I was surprised at how easy it was to shake hands, to promise to write, to agree to meet again on the Outside sometime, somewhere, knowing all the while that it wouldn't happen, that the camaraderie had been in most cases pleasant but not significant, and that we all instinctively understood this—had, in fact, begun to understand it long ago. Only those few inmates with whom I'd shared my first several weeks in jail, in Oakalla's West Wing, right tier, fourth floor, and who were still around finishing off single or multiple sentences, made me feel sad and a little sentimental. We had, after all, shared some fairly turbulent experiences.

Taking leave of someone to transfer to another prison, however, is generally considered much less important than taking leave to quit prison for good. With all the shuffling around that goes on, there's always a reasonable chance you'll be sharing a cell again before you know it, in some other prison up or down the line. So we made only a minimum of fuss. Mieszko made sure all my books were returned and I explained my system of organization in the Tool Room to Jeff, who had reacted quickly to secure my mechanic's job for himself. During the last hour before Lights Out I edited the remaining manuscripts for the Writing Workshop members and talked with them briefly, then cleaned out my locker and threw my remaining knickknacks into a flour sack. By eleven o'clock count my room was bare and alien, ready for the next inmate who would no doubt arrive on the morning truck. I waited for the guard to check the room, then turned out the light and tried to go to sleep. I didn't have much luck.

In the morning the guard who had come in on the truck took me aside for a moment. "I wish ya luck, Andy," he told me kindly, giving me a friendly pat on the back. "And listen, if ya want my advice, get yourself into something sensible like real estate. Forget about all that writing shit; it'll never put bread on your table."

The Chief Officer in charge of the camp was similarly generous. "If you're ever in trouble again after you finish this sentence," he offered as I climbed into the truck, "just get a message to us; we'll be glad to have you back."

FRAGMENT

48

The reason for my transfer from Stave Lake to Pine Ridge has been confirmed; my work release application has apparently been granted in principle and they've assigned me to this camp so I'll be close to Haney's main offices in case the proposal goes through. A work release, if it happens, would permit me to work at an Outside job during the day but require me to return to jail right after work, and to stay there until the job begins again the next day. I'd be permitted to license a vehicle and to park it in the prison parking lot, surrendering my keys, papers and wallet each day to the duty officer at the Pine Ridge office. The prison would deduct eight dollars a day for "room and board."

Basically, I'm pleased with this development, although it's not by any means as benevolent a plan as it may appear. For one thing, the daily shifting from Inside to Outside and back is purportedly extremely hard on the psyche, to which one must add the strain of living under a program full of tension and threat. Any foul-up in the conduct of any inmate who is part of the plan feeds instant negative statistics to its detractors, who are always lurking about waiting to pounce on any innovative experiments launched in the Corrections arena. The wrath of administrators and inmates alike, in other words, constantly hangs over one's head just waiting to be brought down by some unexpected carelessness.

Another unfortunate aspect is that the program is only available in this area through Pine Ridge, which is a somewhat less than contented prison camp at the best of times, and too many of whose guards are loud-mouthed, boorish and cantankerous. I applied for the program only because clearance for a work release is supposed to greatly increase one's chances for parole, and I'm doing everything I can to consolidate my position . . .

While I wait for all the red tape to unravel, I've been informed I'm to repair chain saws at the sawmill operation. I spent most of yesterday digging through all the camp's resources and I couldn't find even a basic complement of tools to do the job; as for spare parts, gaskets or basic maintenance supplies, there are none whatsoever. I expect I'll just keep tearing the most consistently malfunctioning saws apart for parts until I've used up the entire fleet, about which time, with any luck, I should be close enough to my release date to be oblivious to anything but my fixation on that big Main Gate anyway.

Meanwhile, I've been assigned to Hut Three, a twelve-man dormitory heated by an old wood stove set in the middle of the room, and only dimly lit by a few bare light bulbs scattered across the ceiling. The beds are distributed around the room at roughly two-foot intervals; several sets of wooden lockers, for which we've received massive key locks, stand at either end. There are bed-and-locker searches (unannounced of course) about every two to three days, I'm told, and night counts every two hours. I don't know about the searches but I can certainly attest to the counts; every two hours during the past two nights a guard has stomped into the room, his boots thudding so loudly on the floor that I woke up every time.

Another hitch: because the room is so cold (nobody's willing to keep that stove fed all night) and we're only allowed two blankets, many men instinctively pull their blankets up over their heads for more warmth while they sleep. That, however, is against the rules; a guard must see "the neck and head" of each inmate to include him in the count, and as a result the guards are continually yanking the blankets off our heads as they make their two-hour rounds, waking us up again and again. I gather there has been plenty of noise about this, but Security insists that without the blanket rule there is no way to tell whether a body in a bed is real or fake. Since the escape rate is very high in this camp I suppose they have a point, but it's an extremely annoying practice nevertheless and it's going to be very difficult to get used to.

FRAGMENT

49

It's been a very strange day. Late last month I discovered that the girl who was to manage the affairs of my magazine *Contemporary Literature in Translation* in my absence had proven unreliable, and all was in chaos. I made a special, heavily documented application for a temporary pass and yesterday it was accepted; I was permitted a one-day (twelve hours) pass without escort to bring the magazine's affairs (correspondence, subscription files, manuscripts) back up to date. This morning I picked up my pass and my office key (which had been stored in PERSONAL EFFECTS at Haney since my trial), gave the guard at the gate my papers and boarded the next bus into Vancouver, looking neither right nor left, remembering the last time three months ago and not wanting to risk that kind of turmoil again. The bus was almost empty and I sat down in the back, tightly wrapped in my own numbness and studiously not listening to whatever conversation drifted to the rear.

At the office I unlocked the door and found the place empty, thankfully. I checked the files, the scattered piles of paper and the manuscripts and then set to work furiously, in total silence, the thoughts sculling through my head occasionally startling me with unexpected loudness. I worked without stopping until it was done, then jotted a note on a desk pad and left. It was around 4:00 P.M. and I wasn't due back at prison until eight-thirty, but I felt too unreal to see anyone. I boarded the next bus back to Haney and settled into the rear again, feeling somehow as if nothing had happened, as if I'd never left this seat and as if another day had simply been snapped off my ticket and fallen to the floor, insignificant, vacant.

The bus dieseled out of the depot and rasped up Hastings Street, gnarling and chunking from stop to stop; I found myself becoming more and more enveloped in that rough mechanical sound, hiding in its safe meaninglessness, humming and nodding to its rhythm as the bus drove on and on. Eventually I felt myself relax a little; in the sound of the bus there was room for movement, room even for a little play; actually the sound of the bus wasn't a bad rhythm section for snatches of a slightly rheumatic military march, its deep gurgling and chuffing the sound of wheezing old generals describing famous battles they'd almost won, by Jove . . . Then suddenly I heard another sound altogether, a thumping and clanging like the raucous jauntiness of the barrel organs I'd heard in Amsterdam two years ago. I leaned forward and looked out the window to where the sound was coming from, and found we were passing by the Pacific National Exhibition fairgrounds. To my surprise, the exhibition was in full swing.

Then suddenly I realized it was late summer, late August in fact, the time when the fall fairs travel all over B.C.'s lower mainland, when as kids we used to have our last fling before school started again, the new year with all its new anxieties, its apprehensions, its expectations . . . We were passing the Playland part of the fair now; I couldn't see much from the bus except the loop-a-loop, the Ferris wheel and the twisted figure-eight of the roller coaster with its tiny cars swooping up and down over its curves. I'd always enjoyed the roller coaster. The PNE had a huge one, one of the biggest anywhere, it was said. It took up over two acres and as kids we kept hearing rumors that each year two or three people died on it, which made it all the more exciting . . . Suddenly I saw that the bus had stopped at the main Exhibition stop; people were pouring in through the front door, spilling into the seats row after row toward me and I thought, well, what's the difference here or there, if you're going to get crowded into a corner anyway you might as well get yourself into a big one, and I got off the bus.

I crossed the street, passed through the turnstile and then stood hesitating at the periphery for a few moments, looking slightly apprehensively at the hordes milling about the grounds, the whirling, swooping machinery, and then the swirl of the crowd drifted me into its orbit, churning me leisurely through the maze of hawkers and booths, the frenzy and flutter of banners and lights, the patch-quilt turmoil of brightly bustling clothes and hats, past galleries of garish orange and electric-blue poodles and the thickly sweet smell of popcorn, candy floss and hickory-smoked frying wieners.

It was once again as preposterous as I had always remembered it, as seedy and magic and sweaty and wonderful, the most ancient of markets and our oldest ritual feast, and I knew it was good but for me this time it was soundless, like an old silent movie. As I idled along I felt encased in muting glass, the turbulence couldn't touch me, not the urgently beckoning roulette wheel operators, not the program sellers, not the "hurry hurry hurry" men in their sweat-stained worn-out tuxedos. I drifted through them all like a somnolent, ear-plugged swimmer, feeling increasingly cold and lonely, pushing through faces that stretched and widened past me in odd perspectives that made me irrationally nervous. For some reason I kept worrying I'd be recognized.

201

Finally I snagged on the edge of a booth selling ten shots for a dollar, and I watched for a long time as the ducks plunked down and up among their tin-plate bulrushes, endlessly shot and resurrected again as the belt ground round and round, and from somewhere deep down through all the cotton batting I felt a twinge of interest, an instinctual twitch nudging me toward the counter where the guns lay. To break through the languor, the inertia. To kick something into becoming real.

I pressed some money into the attendant's hand and began pumping shots into the ducks, shot after shot, faster and faster, reloading and firing quickly again and again before the sound could die away. Listening. Listening for something to begin to stir, to come alive. Trying for anger, for laughter, for kicks, for hatred; trying for unplugged ears. I poured five dollars' worth of shells into those ducks and it made no difference; I dropped the gun back onto the counter and walked away.

I smiled stupidly, vacantly, at the poodle-carriers and the funny-hat wearers, stopping briefly to watch people having themselves photographed behind the bars of a mock-up jail cell for a dollar and a half. I passed the Ferris wheel and another scattering of refreshment stands and a miniature golf course made of green-painted plywood, and then there was only the loop-a-loop, and the roller coaster fence. I stared at the coaster for a long time.

I'd always liked the roller coaster.

I climbed onto the fence and timed a run; as nearly as I could tell, it took about four minutes for a complete trip. I checked my pockets and found I had six dollars; I climbed down the fence and walked to the ticket counter. "Give me ten," I said to the face behind the chicken wire that looked a trifle astonished in a segmented sort of way. "I've got a large family." At the coaster entrance I showed the man my roll of tickets and explained I'd be using the facilities for a while, and would he leave me undisturbed for ten rides please. He said that would be okay. I waited until a front seat came free, then shoved my tickets in my pocket and settled back.

Nothing much happened as we coasted to the bottom of the first huge hill; I was faintly aware of the chatter of conversation behind me but I wasn't really paying attention; the tow chain had hooked into place and we were being winched higher and higher into the sky, rising slowly through the air up and up until I could see the entire fairgrounds and then the entire city, up and still farther up until I could see the entire harbor and much of the bay, and then suddenly behind me everybody started to scream.

"Damn it, I miss it every time," I barely had time to think and then we were hurtling in a stomach-wrenching plunge toward the ground, the screams behind me rising in a panic-stricken fantailed crescendo, the train sounding like a machine gun over the tracks and the angle so steep the people in the second seat were virtually sitting on my head. We dove to the bottom and lunged up into a right-hand curve, the force of our bottoming-out so enormous that the whole front of the train lifted out of its tracks, hurling us all to the right sides of the seats and almost out of them too.

The screaming behind me was reaching some sort of climax as we looped and swooped, and then we hit the dragon tail. With kidney-twisting contortions the train exploded through a corner and dropped into nothing, everything seemed to come apart in all directions, we were about to end in a million pieces on the bottom down there and then, suddenly caught by the unexpected flick of the tail, we hurled skyward, right out of the tracks and free, launched straight into the evening sun, and above all the shrieking and screeching I heard myself shout very distinctly, "Holy fuck!" And then some safety chain yanked the train back into its grooves and we slammed down onto the seats and over, the tracks spilling us through another loop and another, left and then right ·

203

through berserk impossible angles and then up and down very fast several times until it was all we could do to simply hold desperately onto the safety bars, our bodies connecting only briefly now and then with the seats. I heard myself yell, "Goddamn in tin cans!" and then, "Forty thousand toads!" and then without warning it was over. We coasted up to the loading platform and everybody staggered out. I stayed in my front seat grinning from ear to ear. A minute later we were off again, and this time I didn't miss the apex.

But of course it wasn't nearly as good as the first time, and the third time it was merely boring. After one more ride I got off and give the rest of the tickets to a kid who was hanging around the entrance gate. It didn't matter anyway; my brain felt as if it had been vigorously brushed with a set of stiff bristles, setting the blood coursing a little again and making my body feel as if it had just passed through a bracing shower. I grabbed the next bus that came along and even made it back to Haney with minutes to spare, my cheerful mood calling out a sly expression on the entry guard's face.

"Got the old wick dipped out there?" he suggested with a smirk, riffling through my papers and making appropriate entries in half a dozen books.

"Who the hell's worried about getting it dipped," I lobbed back, taking my papers and heading for the electric doors. "I only just *found* the hootin thing again a couple of hours ago!"

FRAGMENT

I was drinking a cup of tea and talking about this and that with the Protestant padre last night, when we happened to get onto the subject of prison. What was the main irritant, the main condition or privation that most completely symbolized or summed up "being in prison" for me, he wanted to know? What specifically was it that *really* made imprisonment so unpleasant an experience?

I was intrigued by the fact that, despite my almost eight-month imprisonment, I couldn't give him an immediate and specific answer. The more I thought about it, the more I realized that whatever the answer was, it had changed many times during these past eight months and it was still changing, although much more slowly now.

At first, I recalled, it was simply the lack of physical comforts that bothered me, but eventually that kind of irritant fell away and it was my freedom of choice that became the bugbear. I began more and more intensely to resent being ordered about as if I were a child by men who often exhibited those very characteristics themselves, I resented having to live to such a major extent at other men's disposal, and I was annoyed at constantly having to suppress my own wishes so completely as to almost entirely dispense with them. At the same time, the ugliness and brutishness of my surroundings often weighted me down, particularly during my last days in Oakalla when spring was settling in and the birds that had returned to the Prison yard often hopped into the cell-blocks through broken windows, even occasionally darting right into individual cells for bread crumbs, which the inmates always saved from breakfast for that purpose.

Those, however, were the most immediate and thus the least significant irritations, and I soon found them to be the most easily surmountable as well. For a time, while I was doing my sentence up at Stave Lake Camp and was deep into the middle of it, as far from its beginning as its end, I think I even occasionally felt (in a numbed sort of way) no major objection to imprisonment at all; I had learned the ropes, had managed to survive all the standard "fish" mistakes, had developed a reasonably reliable instinct for typical prison dangers and how to avoid them, and was well enough "connected" in the inmate body to keep myself more or less safely above water. The relief at having made it through the often tumultuous first two months was great enough, in fact, to carry me for an equivalent amount of time before the next major vexation set in. When it did, I think it was finally the "real" one, the one most widespread among inmates and also the one most difficult to describe, handle and overcome.

By the time it came, mind you, I had already been in prison for almost four months and the effect had become so cumulatively massive, so overwhelming, that I felt completely lost and buried Inside, totally removed from my past, my family and my friends. It simply took too much effort to remember enough about the world to respond to it. Friends came to visit, of course, but all I could do was talk about what was happening to *me*. I began to forget current connections between people I'd known; I couldn't remember their names and couldn't recall who'd been doing what with whom, and where. It was a little like becoming senile and beginning to mix up the names of your grandchildren.

In those circumstances, then, being in prison slowly began to feel more and more as if I'd been dropped down the hopper of some huge, numbing, unpredictable, implacable and unopposable machine, an apparatus so depersonalized and so unwieldy that even those in control of it didn't ever really expect it to work. It's a common feeling among inmates, and a major source of depression Inside. There isn't, after all, any point in believing much of what you're told once you've discovered that most administrative decisions aren't made on the basis of who you are at all, but merely according to whatever accidental route your papers may take in being shuffled from desk to desk.

For the Corrections system isn't only extraordinarily inefficient, it's also filled to a large extent with personnel who have for all intents and purposes given up, who frankly don't give much of a damn anymore. It isn't even all that surprising; a prison is a pretty unpleasant place to spend one's life, whether one is an inmate or a member of staff, and staff members must annually spend as much as eighteen hundred and forty hours behind bars—about eighty full days a year. Research several years ago monitored a group of newly hired shop instructors who came to prison to teach inmates through an industrial rehabilitation program and who, at the outset, were eager, full of ideas and very optimistic about their jobs. Two years later a combination of tests and interviews showed the group to be sadly depleted, out of ideas and effectively "institutionalized." In addition, it was found that their functional vocabulary level had dropped by an average of 50 percent. It's hard to resist the steady onslaught of chronic inmate discontent, public censure and statistics forever proving that your every new idea or plan is failing.

It is the combination of this administration lethargy and inmate distress, of staff members who no longer care and inmates who are desperate to get out but can only make their applications and appeals through that same staff, which finally leads to the sense of futility and dejection that permeates every prison in which I've done my time, and, without doubt, every prison in North America. It's the source of most of the cynicism and hypocrisy that pervade modern-day jails, and it's ultimately another major reason for the Corrections system's failure to solve its part of the Crime Cycle problem. Because it's all very well to try out one new rehabilitative idea after another (invented and drawn up almost exclusively by nonprison personnel), but if the same tired, fed-up prison staff are used to implement such ideas each time, the failure of those ideas is a foregone conclusion. Nobody realizes this as clearly as the inmates who are serving their time under that staff, and by the time I'd done four months in prison, that realization had begun to make me feel pretty hopeless too.

FRAGMENT

51

More thoughts on imprisonment:

Sometimes, I must admit, I am thoroughly puzzled by this strange and somehow perverse (at least from an inmate's point of view) agreement between society and the offender; society proposes to consider prison the most dishonorable and tragic place for a man to be, and the inmate, astonishingly enough, agrees to go along with the proposal, consenting in effect to value his experience by the very yardstick with which society is rapping his knuckles. In order for imprisonment to be truly dreadful, in other words, it requires the full cooperation of the prisoner himself, and I've often been truly amazed at how willingly most inmates offer that cooperation.

Obviously, most inmates are quite unaware of any such complicity, although virtually every inmate I know tacitly accepts the unspoken premise that he is being part of a bad experience, one of the worst on society's menu, and that he has in some irredeemable way failed or lost. And yet I'm willing to bet that if an act of Parliament were passed (or a new social attitude developed) such that "as of today, being in prison will be considered honorable and fun," fully half of all inmates would promptly begin to have a good time. Because one can't ignore the fact that many inmates know no other life; they have their friends, their reputations, their culture and their frames of reference Inside, and couldn't possibly find another world that would accept their values and credentials half as readily. In a fair number of cases something like this has already occurred, in that some inmates, either consciously or subconsciously, have decided that prison is their world, and that the negative image it carries is relevant only to those who intend to return to the "straight society" Outside. These inmates have no intention of doing so.

FRAGMENT

When I got to Stave Lake five months ago I had an idea; the idea of being driven to total desperation, of being pushed so hard that even my language and vision would change; of discovering what I really needed to stay alive. What I eventually unearthed was both disappointing and reassuring; disappointing because the typical North American miracle I was after (instant; just add water) didn't happen in that way; reassuring because my language and vision *did* change in time, albeit slowly and with many hesitations. I found I was too resilient a cynic to ever totally despair and too entrenched an artist to ever become totally bored, and I could live on almost nothing; for short times on nothing at all but a little food.

What I was and what I needed had proven to be only a small, durable core inside me, like a small dried fig. Whatever havoc had been wreaked on the person I thought I was, began to feel like useful pruning, as if a lot of unnecessary, confused and even absurd excess had been pared off. The result, therefore, was nothing at all like bitterness but something more akin to cheerfulness (if one can imagine such a thing in prison); I felt that peculiar spiritual freedom, that lyric light-headedness one commonly associates with fasts. I became virtually uninsultable, unoffendable, even unblackmailable by my own desires or those of another human being: conversely, it took less and less to put me in a good mood and to keep me there. A smuggled-in cigar. Cherries (sodden, ancient, but nonetheless cherries) for dessert. Evidence that someone had understood exactly what I'd been trying to explain. A good chess game.

I discovered also, during my brief period of work release (which finally did come through), when the differences between Insiders and Outsiders seemed particularly pronounced, that those differences were in fact misleading, a fallacy. As I listened with increasing interest and curiosity to the ways in which my cell mates understood themselves and each other, I began to realize that we were not only part of the same world, but also, in the final analysis, part of the same quest. We were traveling for all intents and purposes in the same direction, which was into the world to find ourselves warm places to live in and warm people to live with, and somehow in whatever wisdom we achieved, there had to be room for us all, or it was pointless. That was at first the hardest and then eventually the easiest idea to understand. Whatever we presumed to understand had to explain both the best and the worst of us, the idiots and the geniuses, the confused and the attentive, both prisoners and guards. In an environment as polarized as a prison, that's a difficult mouthful to swallow, but it's probably the only place in which I could have swallowed it. The opposite view in a place like this is so obviously too easy, it immediately gives itself away.

FINIS

When I got out of prison (after just under eight months' time), the release (parole) was so sudden and unheralded, I didn't even have time to call a friend to pick me up. On September 26, 1975, the papers abruptly arrived and two hours later I was walking through that big Main Gate into the parking lot, free. It was very strange. For months I had imagined that moment, had dreamed about it and yearned for it. Now this was it, and I felt—almost nothing. A kind of numbness. A theoretical rather than actual pleasure. I hitched a ride to Mission and walked the mile from the main road to the house, feeling remote and slightly tired. I unlocked the door, walked inside and looked around. It was pretty much as I remembered it. The books. The furniture. I sat down in an armchair, not in the least inclined to phone anyone. I felt somehow displeased. I couldn't puzzle it out.

Eventually I realized it was the house, in a way. I'd been away for an incredibly long time, I felt like men must have felt coming home from war, I felt totally changed—and I suppose in some unthinking way I expected to find my surroundings changed as well. The thought occurred to me that I would probably have to move, to find myself a new house for new reasons, but I didn't have time to come to a decision about it then; I was flying to Montreal to a writers' conference I hadn't expected to be able to attend and had barely enough time to sleep in the place for a night before I left.

Finally it was in that city, just drifting through the streets being jostled by the great chattering crowds who paid no attention to me at all as they rushed along, that I started to thaw out. It didn't come all at once, rather in isolated little bursts, in small explosions of joy that overwhelmed and shook me like inverted fits of chill; hell, I felt like tearing out the telephone poles, whooping it up like a frenzied T.V. Indian, leaping onto postboxes to give long roaring speeches, chasing huge herds of thundering buffalo through Montreal's streets—it was fabulous beyond belief.

Impulsively I decided I'd have to allow myself at least one of those unrulinesses or I'd come completely unglued. I searched around until I found an empty alley and let fly—a long, high-pitched all-out *yahooooooooo* that should have brought the walls crashing down but which, as far as I could see, went entirely unheard in the general downtown traffic din. I ruled I'd have to be satisfied with that, turned about and drifted on, feeling marvelously calm and mellow.

When I returned home several weeks later and settled down to work conducting writing workshops for inmates (at Matsqui Penitentiary, Abbotsford, B.C.) and working on this book, the problem of the house was of no further consequence. It had simply become a useful wooden device that kept the rain off my desk and the wind from playing havoc with the manuscripts.